PLAY IT
FORWARD

D0112451

Praise for Joan Barnes and *Play It Forward*

"A raw, rare, and illuminating touchstone for future generations of women to sort out how to achieve success on their own terms."
—**Elana Yonah Rosen**, chief development officer of the
Nasdaq Entrepreneurial Center

"Inspirational and very informative. You get a feel for how to really start a business with little money, and you see that it is possible to have the courage and determination to confront major personal challenges in the midst of building a successful business."
—**Phillip Moffitt**, president of Life Balance Institute,
author of *Emotional Chaos to Clarity*

"Joan's enthusiasm, passion, and wit are contagious, and her intellect is razor sharp. She has gifted us a thoughtful book that will encourage and educate women of all ages."
—**Karen Behnke**, founder of Juice Beauty

"When Yoga Works acquired YogaStudios from Joan Barnes, we bought more than a business; we inherited a great culture with a dynamic community spirit from a visionary who saw the possibilities and the boundless potential in each of us."
—**Phil Swain**, CEO of Yoga Works

"Joan Barnes blessed my family with a magic carpet ride. As successful franchisees for 25 years, my parents raised me in Gymboree's joyous environment, living balanced lives. Now, my son is blossoming there too. Joan's dynamic entrepreneurism inspires me to build my business and grow my family. Her story is one for the ages."
—**Rachel Pally**, founder and CEO of Rachelpally.com

"Joan Barnes is as provocative as she is inspiring. Her story and success keenly highlight the paradoxes of strength and vulnerability. She leaves the audience moved and wanting more."
—**Stephanie Brenner Kirksey**, senior director at Capital One

PLAY IT FORWARD

From Gymboree to the Yoga Mat and Beyond

Joan Barnes AND **Michael J. Coffino**

AN AGATE IMPRINT

CHICAGO

Printed in the United States

Library of Congress Cataloging-in-Publication Data

Names: Barnes, Joan, author. | Coffino, Michael J., author.
Title: Play it forward : from Gymboree to the yoga mat and beyond / by Joan Barnes and Michael J. Coffino.
Description: Chicago : B2 Books/Agate, [2016]
Identifiers: LCCN 2015050650 (print) | LCCN 2016007318 (ebook) | ISBN 9781572841901 (paperback) | ISBN 1572841907 (paperback) | ISBN 9781572847750 (ebook) | ISBN 1572847751 (ebook)
Subjects: LCSH: Barnes, Joan | Gymboree (Corporation) | Physical education teachers--United States--Biography. | Businesswomen--United States--Biography. | Physical fitness centers--United States. | Movement education--United States. | BISAC: BIOGRAPHY & AUTOBIOGRAPHY / Business. | FAMILY & RELATIONSHIPS / Parenting / General. | HEALTH & FITNESS / Yoga.
Classification: LCC GV333.B37 A3 2016 (print) | LCC GV333.B37 (ebook) | DDC 796.092--dc23
LC record available at http://lccn.loc.gov/2015050650

10 9 8 7 6 5 4 3 2 1   16 17 18 19 20

B2 is an imprint of Agate Publishing. Agate books are available in bulk at discount prices.
agatepublishing.com

The conversations and events recounted in this book are substantially as Joan Barnes remembers and perceives them, taking into account the more than four decades this book covers. While the authors made reasonable efforts to be precise, conversations are not presented as word-for-word transcriptions, but rather have been retold to capture the essence of what was said. Similarly, some events may not be described or sequenced with precise accuracy but are also presented in accordance with best recollection. Finally, to protect individuals' privacy, the authors changed some of the names of people in this book.

*For my daughters, Meegan and Cecily, and my grandchildren,
Ethan, Alex, and Edie Mae, whose life and love elevate me every day*

*For Adeline Helen Barbarisi and Irving Morris Coffino, for instilling
in me the confidence that my reach has no bounds*

∞∞∞∞∞∞∞∞∞∞∞

We tell ourselves stories in order to live.

JOAN DIDION

I WAS IN THE KITCHEN, slicing apples at 9:00 a.m. in full-throttle preparation for our annual family Seder dinner, when the landline rang. I assumed it was one of the usual suspects invited to the Seder calling to bow out, ask to bring a friend, or clarify a food assignment. Or one of my daughters, who liked to check in with me early each morning. I doubted it was a solicitor—too early even for one of them.

When I glanced at the caller ID, however, I saw "Gymboree." *Huh?* My mind went blank and, staring at the phone, I dropped the knife I was holding. There had been no contact with the company I founded for longer than I could remember, and I was at once curious and anxious about the reason for the call.

I cupped the receiver with both hands, cleared my throat for some semblance of presence, and as nonchalantly as I could, uttered "Hello," with a tinge of curious question mark.

The corresponding voice introduced himself as Mark Breitbard, the new Gymboree CEO. It was 2013, 22 years since I had been the Gymboree CEO and 37 since I'd founded the company. Six CEOs had succeeded me, and not one had ever contacted me.

I told Mark he had caught me off guard, and in my nervousness disclosed that I was awash in kitchen duty for a Seder. He chuckled warmly and proceeded to delight me with an account of his own upcoming Seder, from which I also learned that we were neighbors in Mill Valley, in Marin County, California, who lived only two minutes away from each other. These coincidences and personal tidbits dissolved my initial apprehension, replaced by easy conversational flow and a comfortable connection.

Mark told me he wanted to understand the company's heritage better and honor its legacy. He hoped I would make time to meet so he could learn more about me, about the inspiration that spawned the business, and about how we built an international powerhouse from humble beginnings. He was hungry to know about the early years, our reason for expanding beyond the play program to retail, and much more. He added that, in addition to meeting with him, he hoped I would spend time with his management team and even speak to the entire company. As the new steward of Gymboree, he felt strongly that bringing the founder home and instilling the history of the company in the entire staff were imperatives. We agreed to meet soon for breakfast.

When the call ended, I paused to allow this unanticipated encounter to settle. Seder preparation could simmer on the back burner for a few minutes. I was transported back to the Gymboree adrenaline rush days, when the thrill of the entrepreneurial ride had hooked me. I visualized in rapid succession various images from a time gone by: attentive teachers overseeing giggly toddlers running from activity to activity, stacks of signature colorful playwear perched on bleacher-like shelves at retail stores, and a collage of the beautiful and loyal colleagues with whom I had shared this major part of my life. I felt a smile spread over my face and my heartbeat speed up. I wandered to the living room window seat and perched on the narrow cushioned bench. Then something stopped me short.

All of a sudden, I was not sure, frankly, what I was feeling. While happy to hear from Gymboree, I was reminded of the sense of slight I'd felt when no prior CEO had contacted me for so long. I became uneasy about the possibility that these and more unresolved feelings would surface from my Gymboree departure. I wondered whether a reconnection to Gymboree would enhance my life, or be no more than a passing event, or drag me back to a time that I had left far behind. I realized I couldn't afford the time right now to drill down any deeper. Seder dinner preparation took precedence, and this unplanned turn of events would have to wait.

By next afternoon, my focus shifted to the upcoming meeting with Mark. I knew he was not after what he could freely learn from ready-made Google or YouTube exploration, but rather my view of the mysteries of why some companies, in the face of challenge, find or redefine themselves. I revisited various turning points in Gymboree's history, beginning with the initial idea to form the first play center, how I handled early expansion opportunities and critical decisions, and how Gymboree evolved into a global network of franchised play programs and company-owned retail stores. I wanted to help Mark, contribute to Gymboree, and manage to have a positive personal experience.

As it turned out, the breakfast went well. We bounced from subject to subject seamlessly, just as we had on our initial call. Mark showed genuine curiosity and he asked questions like a seasoned journalist. I sensed he was focused on how to thread the company's heritage into the future he was leading it toward. I felt excited for Gymboree.

Mark invited me to join him and his management team at a business retreat in Napa in a few weeks. I agreed to join them for lunch and prepared diligently for the meeting, poring over my records and contacting former colleagues to ask questions and obtain additional documents, including press clippings and archival materials. Lacking a given agenda, I didn't know what they would ask or what I was expected to say. I wanted to be prepared for almost anything and meet expectations, whatever they were.

The self-induced research project fueled an even deeper and more powerful journey into the past. As I traveled back in time, I realized how vast my knowledge was about starting and building a business. More so, I saw in vivid detail how my incredible Gymboree voyage had propelled me down a bump-filled road that, in the end, exposed me to myself in ways that yielded deep self-awareness. In the current light of day, what I'd learned, both professionally and personally, had been incalculably valuable. As I anticipated the Napa meeting, I became excited about contributing to the rejuvenation project Mark was spearheading, and hoped that a vibrant connection to the past could help pave the way for a glorious Gymboree future.

The lunch meeting in Napa was dynamic and wide-ranging. The management group was well prepared and asked probing questions. Their palpable, genuine interest in the company heritage impressed me, and the binders of vintage photos and brochures I brought for my modest dog-and-pony show fascinated them. The opportunity to feel, once again, a part of the ongoing Gymboree story and family, and to recount early history, with all its color and nuance, moved me. And the respect, deference, and heartfelt warmth I received was just as stirring.

During a break, a group of predominantly young female executives encircled me. They wanted to hear how I had handled the balance of raising young children, having a personal life, and managing the extreme demands of Gymboree. Their inquiries reflected the ongoing struggles working women have with family life, demanding professions and businesses, and self-care. Their genuine openness impressed me, as did the sense they communicated of how far the conversation had come over the decades, and yet how similar the internal struggles continued to be. Noting that this was not an ideal circumstance for a forum on this weighty topic, and not wanting to be glib, I briefly touched on how vitally important it is for each woman to find answers that are right for her, and to be wary of external pressures and expectations that could throw them off course and wreak havoc with their attempts to stay true to their core selves.

Mark formalized the invitation for me to speak to the entire company at its annual kickoff meeting in San Francisco. I told him it was important I have at my side my "Origin Team," the inner circle of colleagues who had been with me for each step as the company grew and prospered. I explained that we had run the business as a team, and any such reconnection in front of the company would not ring true without them. He agreed. I extended the invitations, which were all enthusiastically accepted, save one former colleague with an unavoidable schedule conflict.

I was, as I later learned, a "surprise" at the annual meeting. And, as a surprise to me, Mark also used the meeting to introduce a new annual employee award: *The Joan Barnes Entrepreneurial and Vision Award*. I was beyond flattered; I was floored. And, personal feelings aside, in addition to honoring my legacy, Mark also hoped to embed more deeply the value of innovation and entrepreneurial spirit in the Gymboree company culture.

I made my presentation to the assembled company, engaged in questions and answers with Mark, and then took questions from employees. The scene reminded me of TV shows that reunite long-lost relatives after countless years of separation, or introduce a family member others never knew existed. This event affected me powerfully, not merely because of the personal attention and accolades—which felt good, for sure—but also because of how the reconnection spawned such pervasive warmth and enthusiasm.

While we mingled after the formal presentations, dozens of people introduced themselves to me. Each shared a vignette and expressed heartfelt appreciation for the opportunity to meet the founder of the company they cherished, and to learn more about its legacy. Some had acquired their first home because of the job security they enjoyed at Gymboree. Many had worked at the company for more than ten years and felt there was no better place. They loved learning about how so many women had blossomed as an outgrowth of the original culture. Some said they had left Gymboree to work elsewhere, only to return because of its special feel and inclusiveness. This was corporate family at its finest.

Six months later, Gymboree asked me to make the ultimate back-to-the-future expedition. I accompanied Mark; the franchise division president, Jill Johnston; and the whole franchise team to Las Vegas in November 2013 to attend—again as a surprise guest—the annual Gymboree franchise convention. After I was introduced, I was stunned to be greeted with a standing ovation. I was unable to hold back tears of joy.

It was heart-stopping to be embraced this way by these women, many of whom still teach with passion and pride the very Gymboree program they proudly introduced to their communities some 30 years ago! Their classes today might include the toddler children of the kids they taught back then. The contagious sense of passion, soul, and continuity all combined to knock me out.

And, when I thought my capacity for celebration was saturated, I was introduced to the international franchisees, some of
whom believed so strongly in the Gymboree mission that, against
stiff political and social odds, they had courageously invested
their hearts and dollars to forge programs in Saudi Arabia, Paki-
stan, Honduras, Malaysia, Qatar, Turkey, Argentina, Kazakhstan,
Thailand, Ukraine, Singapore, India, China, Colombia, and nearly
40 other countries. What a joy to experience the collective expression, spoken through so many different languages, of a global
brand that went far beyond mere merchandise. I could not get
enough of their stories and took advantage of as many photo opportunities as possible. It was all glorious.

I once compared our Gymboree organizational chart to the
rings of Saturn, orbiting the globe, rather than a traditional flat
flow chart. I was awed by the potency of what had once been just
a single scrappy idea about which a few of us cared so much.

Those experiences of reconnecting with Gymboree, on top of
repeated requests for "your book" at speaking engagements, and
the encouragement of many, including my coauthor, moved me
to write this book. I hesitated at first, feeling self-conscious and
presumptuous. I reminded myself, however, that my personal
and professional journey taught me many things, not the least
of which is that telling our stories illuminates our self-awareness
and, when bravely and transparently told, these stories can have
a meaningful impact on others. Someone very dear to me and
now gone once said: "The more we tell our stories, the more we
define ourselves." While the contexts and audiences might vary,

our stories should be told, as each holds importance beyond our own lives; if those stories go untold, we can lose the opportunity they present to benefit others.

I have learned that aspiring entrepreneurs, engaged young people, and so many others crave insights, role models, and straight talk about the challenges involved in building a business, not only financially, but in achieving a balanced life in tune with our personal values. I wanted to recount how, after an extraordinary roller coaster ride in building a major international business, I eventually aligned my inner life with my outward success.

My fervent hope is that you will find parts of yourself in my story, and however dissimilar our life experiences, you might find value in the interconnecting themes of entrepreneurial spirit and passion, meeting failure and setback head-on without losing hope, the power of street smarts, instinct, tenacity, and truth-telling, and the journey of reinvention. Reading my story, you can join me in facing that mirror together.

CHAPTER 1

Facing a Reboot on All Fronts

ON WEDNESDAY, MARCH 31, 1993, Gymboree, the company I had founded almost 20 years earlier in 1974 in a local, makeshift community center, and gradually built into a powerful global brand, enjoyed a historic initial public offering on NASDAQ.

As the first day of public trading ended, lead investment banker Goldman Sachs proudly announced that the share price had spiked 58 percent. The IPO poured $43 million into the Gymboree coffers. A parade of early investment houses, the management team, the board members, and the IPO lawyers all celebrated in disparate locations throughout the nation. Investment bankers in New York, San Francisco, and Boston splashed the news in prestigious business publications nationwide. In Silicon

Valley, our initial venture capital firm colleagues clinked champagne glasses and toasted a resounding victory: Gymboree had catapulted to number two in their portfolio, second only to Sun Microsystems. From a single day of trading, their initial Gymboree investment had swelled nineteen times. Many became wealthy overnight, some millionaires and even more multimillionaires. Just like that.

I had started Gymboree with $3,000 in seed money, a personal need, and a hunch, operating a few days a week out of a social hall with minimal equipment. The unassuming first play centers, featuring age-appropriate activities for parents and young children to play together, allowed moms like me to spend meaningful time with other moms and their toddlers. The company addressed the personal feelings of isolation I felt as a young mom and provided an outlet for creativity, mine and that of many others, as it grew to become an interlocking global network of franchised play-and-music centers and company-owned retail clothing stores for kids.

Celebration seemed not merely appropriate, but downright required. In the life of every entrepreneur, an IPO deserves a prominent place as a career highlight. More than just an emblem of financial success, for a founder, an IPO is a defining legacy event. As career trophies go, I could have collected none grander in the two decades-plus of my subsequent life experience.

I was, however, nowhere near Wall Street that fine spring day. I was not at the Gymboree helm. I was not sitting at my desk awash in flattering telephone interviews. I was not participating in any of the festivities or basking in the limelight of this momentous happening. In fact, I knew nothing about that grand IPO moment as it was happening.

I was a thousand metaphorical miles away, as I had departed Gymboree a few years earlier in shambles. And, despite what I hoped appeared to the world as an orderly transition, I was wallowing in the scattered debris of a major crash and burn as I emerged from a long-term live-in treatment program. I was still too tender to enjoy the joyous distillation of the preceding two decades of hard work and achievement, or even care for that matter. My priority was recovery and renewal.

Here were some of the blunt facts I was facing. I had under my belt a hard-fought and well-earned abstinence from bulimia. I was no longer the darling "Gymboree Lady." The ink on my divorce papers was barely dry after 25 years of marriage. The house we'd shared—along with my long-amassed collection of American country antiques, each representing a cherished experience and together constituting a canvas of personal expression—now belonged to my ex-husband in accordance with our marital settlement agreement. I had neither career nor home. Both of my daughters were now away at college. My life accoutrements were the two nondescript suitcases of clothes with which I had left California for what I had assumed would be a 30-day treatment program. I hadn't imagined I would spend another year in a long-term extended care program 3,000 miles from my California home and, then, still not feeling steady enough following that year in treatment, elect to rent an apartment near the treatment facility to stay close to my recovery routine and new allies. I faced a reboot on all fronts.

The day after the IPO—April Fools' Day—I was in California. I was visiting, mind you, to test-drive my psyche for a possible return to the Golden State. That day I was alone for my maiden eating-out voyage. The composite residue of my eating-disorder recovery was fresh in my consciousness. I was respectful and cautious.

I selected the California Cafe in Los Gatos for my reentry meal for a particular reason. The restaurant had recently hosted Bill Clinton and Al Gore on the campaign trail, and I was an avid supporter of this political team. Perhaps, I mused, I could enjoy a vicarious energy transfusion from their recent visit. Regardless, it was the kind of outing I used to do just for fun. I was hoping that, finally, the time had returned for some lightheartedness after all my years of work. Shouldn't she be able to feel fun again, this new woman I had become?

I arrived at the restaurant, parked, and entered. The smells I always considered uniquely California—sage, bay laurel, juniper, and mock orange—were intoxicating. Oh, how I had missed their bouquet. I requested a comfortable booth. I relished being alone that day. One consequence of recovery was how increasingly copacetic I felt with my own company. I noticed that across from my table sat a younger group. They were upbeat, absorbed in each other's company, Silicon Valley would-be world conquerors. Their engaged, energetic dialogue was brisk, and made me curious. The tone of the banter was familiar, as bursts of laughter trumped all their chatting. I missed those days. So, naturally, I overheard, or in truth eavesdropped on, their conversation.

Then my ears pricked up.

"A local company, not a tech one, went public yesterday," the sole woman said to her male companions.

"Which?"

"Gymboree. Yes, yes, Gymboree."

I thought I must have misheard her. But no, the sound of "Gymboree" reverberated and then trailed off. There was no mistake. If this was not synchronicity, then what? My mind spun in reverse, reeling back memories of my 20-year-long Gymboree life: happy children in play centers, my favorite women franchisees, designing the retail stores, vibrant brainstorming meetings, cherished colleagues, the flattering and attentive buzz of media, and on and on.

Before long, I returned to my restaurant reality. Realizing I was now staring into space, I forced my eyes to rest on the Bill Clinton Favorites menu displayed on the white linen tablecloth. I scanned the menu choices. *Maybe I'll order the rack of lamb,* I thought. My menu focus did not last. I had to know if my imagination had run amuck. The waitress approached.

"May I have a few more minutes? The menu has so many delightful choices," I cajoled her while I scanned for a newspaper.

"Of course, no rush, take your time."

We exchanged smiles, hers genuine and soft. I noticed her curly red hair, like mine. She was petite, probably the same age as one of my daughters.

I slipped out of my booth, and there, next to the hostess station on a rattan bench, I spotted an unread copy of the *New York
Times*. I picked it up and started scanning.

It was all true. The business page of the *Times* heralded the
Gymboree IPO announcement. The *Times* reported that "investors went wild over" Gymboree. Demand for shares was so great
that underwriters reset the target price upward by almost 40
percent, which spawned a buying "frenzy" that drove the initial
offering price up by 58 percent, and prompted lead underwriter
Goldman Sachs to add 200,000 shares to the offering. In fact,
stock bidding was so "fierce" that venture capitalists and company insiders sold 1 million shares to the public, an IPO rarity.

The *Times* article also provided specifics about the growing
size of the company, its pervasive locations across the country,
current expansion plans, and, impressively, recent financial performance featuring sales that had "skyrocketed" to $86.3 million
in the most recent fiscal year, almost 10 times from four years
previously.

My heartbeat stepped up as I read. The article was powerful and laudatory. Although the story mentioned that the company was "founded as a sole proprietorship in 1976," it made no
mention of me, the founder. Gymboree, however, was a market
mover, it seemed, and its IPO portended a new era for consumer
venture IPOs.

That such a momentous day as a Gymboree IPO might arrive
had never flashed across my mental screen, even for a subliminal
instant. Now, it seemed surreal. Had you queried me years before

how I might react to such news, I suspect I would have gushed immense pride. Now, on learning that the company I founded and nearly killed myself trying to make a success had fulfilled the dream that most every entrepreneur covets, I felt largely unfazed. A little singed, perhaps, that my contribution seemed a mere anonymous passing reference, unworthy of journalistic acknowledgment. (Yes, now *there* was some good news: my ego appeared to be intact!)

In the shadow of the IPO announcement, no one from Gymboree—with the exception of a former Gymboree colleague and dear friend, Bud Jacob, long gone from the company, and my mentor Stuart Moldaw—called me. Out of sight, out of mind, I imagined. Both Bud and Stu congratulated me and also reminded me that I would "come into some money" after the initial lock-up period of six months, but I was numb to the financial impact.

When I had driven through Los Gatos before lunch in search of an appropriate new place to live, my mind was set on my future rather than my past. Los Gatos is a cute enclave south of San Jose, boasts nice hiking trails, and is near the ocean and UC Santa Cruz, where my younger daughter, Cecily, went to college at the time. My older daughter, Meegan, was at California College of Arts & Crafts in Oakland about an hour away, although she aspired to head to New York soon to intern for the hip *Paper* magazine. I subscribe to the roots and wings theory of parenting (know from where you come and know where you need to fly), which seemed to have favored the girls. I breathed easy, believing that they seemed well on their own life paths, and that my troubles and years away had not affected them too badly. I anticipated that the early love-glue would stick; at least, I hoped so. Nonetheless, I was looking to my daughters to make up some of the lost mommy time I suffered while healing in Florida. Being in Los Gatos would allow me to be close to both of them while I launched my personal restart.

I had a sense of cautious readiness for a return to California. Time would tell if the healthy roots set down in faraway Florida were potted deep enough not to snap when the inevitable Pacific storms of hard reminders and bad patterns hit me. After all, on that sunny April Fools' Day, I was already weathering a pretty hefty storm with the IPO news.

I put the paper down, returned to my table, straightened my back, decided yes on the Bill Clinton lamb, and added an Al Gore little gems salad to my order. I cherished my developing inner strength like a newborn, in the same passionate way I had once cared for young Gymboree as it began to grow. I wondered what it would have been like to share the victorious day of the IPO announcement with that early core group of committed colleagues with whom I built Gymboree. Before long, I was back to feeling calm, with a prevailing sense of contentment about my life direction. Add to that a dash of cosmic timing involved in this return. Los Gatos was off to a good start.

The road to this point had been tumultuous, replete with compelling crossroads and invaluable course corrections. Yet without its constant obstacles, the discovery of life's real treasures would have eluded me. I knew one thing for certain: the highs I once craved had yielded to an appreciation of steady joy. I no longer embraced the delusion that I could defy gravity. I had stepped down from the high wire for good, and faced my new frontiers with cheer and optimism. I anticipated my future with renewed vigor. I had come a long way.

CHAPTER 2

ooooooooooooooooooooooooooooo

OK, Mama!

IT WAS A ROUTINE DAY IN APRIL 1973, when the phone rang.

"Hello, is this Joan Barnes?" the nurse practitioner asked.

"Yes, it is," I answered eagerly.

"Well, Joan, I have good news and bad news for you."

This tender bedside manner was not the best way for us to get started. I had called my ob-gyn for the results of a pregnancy test. Now my mind raced.

I wanted to be outside in the air. I felt suffocated and short of breath. I started to pace in our little house, which overlooked the Croton-on-Hudson reservoir some 35 miles north of Manhattan. The short phone cord, however—remember those?—jerked me back. The reference to "bad news" echoed inside my head.

What could be bad news? Genetic diseases? How could they have an inkling of stuff like that from a basic pregnancy test? Aren't the results merely positive or negative? I realized I didn't know how this worked. Could it be Down syndrome? Something else? What?

"OK, let's start with the bad news, please," I replied. "I like to end on a high, if that is possible."

"Well, Joan, the test results confirm you are pregnant. That's the bad news. But the good news, according to the recent Supreme Court ruling, is that we are now permitted to schedule abortions. We can do them in our office; the procedure is quick and painless. Would you like to schedule one?"

Huh? Schedule an abortion? Right then? *Ever?* Slow this train down, please!

I was transported back to the dark days when my girlfriends, faced with a similar dilemma, took severe measures. Before the early 1970s, if a woman had an unplanned pregnancy, she likely started a family. Some, though, "went away" to have their babies and then give them up for adoption—all very hush-hush. Still others, however, like some of my college girlfriends, took more drastic, illicit action. The memories of hand-holding trips with girlfriends to visit marginal doctors in sleazy outposts are as vivid today as they were then. My college sisters hoped these sketchy characters would terminate their unwanted pregnancies. The procedures were borderline primitive, including an after-procedure pill that seemed the size of a small hard-boiled egg. We each did our best to be stoic and mature, but in reality we were scared shitless kids, including me, who was not even pregnant. I refused to think the worst as my friends squeezed my hand for dear life, eyes welling with terror, as they drifted off under what I prayed were the short-term effects of a strong analgesic. We did what we felt we had to do in those days.

Well, I reminded myself, that was then and this was now. Three months before, days after I turned 26, the Supreme Court had transformed the family-planning landscape with its land-mark ruling *Roe v. Wade*. The decision was a major event of our time. Yet despite being mindful of this historic decision, it hadn't made my life any clearer. While my husband, Bill Barnes, and I had always planned on a family, a pregnancy was not part of any current life-plan. We had ample time for that. For the foreseeable future, we were happily immersed in sowing our oats and estab-lishing our young life together.

On the phone, I was speechless. The nurse barely knew me. *The bad news?* Why did she presume this was bad news for me? Who wrote her lines in this script? I terminated the call in anger and fear. *Abortion? No.* I wanted my baby, didn't I?

I couldn't call anyone until Bill and I had a chance to talk. Bill, however, was inaccessible in that pre-cellphone era, doing research on a deadline for a freelance journalism project. Who else could I talk to? Certainly not my mother. She and I didn't have that kind of relationship, and never had. Since forever, it seemed, I couldn't wait to move beyond her control and the still waters of surburban Chicago, where I was raised among the privileged upper middle class. Living in New York since coming to college had been so liberating. No, Mom was not an option. While Dad and I were pals, and he was my champion, talking to him about my pregnancy would embarrass us both. After all, I had sworn my mom to secrecy when I first got my period, and for all I knew he might believe I still hadn't gotten it. Well, probably not—but in those days, in my family at least, my brother and my dad stayed miles away from the taboo-laden feminine frontier.

I had to endure the aftermath of the ob-gyn call alone until Bill came home, an eternity later. I couldn't contain myself. While his vintage briefcase was still dangling from his shoulder, I announced we must talk—NOW. He backed away from our embrace, alarmed. He knew me well enough to intuit that something serious was amiss. He put his hand up like a traffic cop and silently nodded, signaling assent, and walked our two excited dogs to their pen. He sensed that whatever was going down would not brook interruptions from our innocent canines. He came in, took my hand, and walked us to the porch, where we sat together on one of two large floor cushions. We had no couch in that home, only a rope hammock hanging from our ceiling and a few hippy-style hassocks strewn in our tiny living room. Our artwork was a collage of orange-painted plywood boards nailed to the wall, our version of a contemporary mural. We prized our little artistic cabin in the country, our first home.

I blurted it out: "BB, I am pregnant—we are pregnant."

I burst out sobbing and he held me tightly. Neither of us uttered a word for a long time. We were feeling our way. Then Bill pulled away gently, one arm around my shoulder and his other hand in mine. The connection was secure, an electrical circuitry traveling between our bodies, hearts connected.

"We've imagined our children, played around with possible names, joked about whose personality traits they might have, your zest, my brilliance. . . ." His light touch and self-effacing manner brought me my first smile since the nurse's call. He continued, "But . . ."

I pulled back. That word; I hated that word. It always discounted or canceled what it followed. I dislodged my hand from his.

". . . don't you think we need to be where we want to live before we take such a bold step?"

This was more statement than question. He spoke about the need to regain stability after his recent departure from *Time* magazine and how he was absorbed in replanting his stake in journalism, and blah, blah, blah about timing, and so on.

I cut him off. "So, you want me to have an abortion? A fucking legal abortion?"

I got up and bolted toward the bathroom, grabbed my tape player on the way, then locked myself in and ran a bath, blasting Crosby, Stills & Nash's "Wooden Ships." I cried and cried until the tub began to overflow.

After a while, Bill knocked and begged me to let him in. I relented and unlocked the door. I looked up from the bath with swollen eyes and puffy cheeks, and said softly, "I do not want to abort our baby. I want to start our family now. We can figure this out."

His bluer-than-blue eyes welled up with their own tears. I could tell he was processing at record pace; we both were. He smiled and nodded. Reaching for me, he washed my back. Several silent moments passed. And as I really began to appreciate how much I had asked of him in such a short time, he smiled gently and said, "OK, Mama!"

That night we chose to read in bed after a light supper and dispense with further talk about family. We had drawn a very broad and deep line in the sand regarding the future direction of our lives. That was more than enough for then.

Throughout the next day I refinished antiques for the little shop I'd opened, called Hindsight, on the roadside that abutted our house. Before getting started, I hung the SHUT sign: no customers today. Lost in my reverie, I needed process-time to feel my way through what had happened between Bill and me, and to ponder the inevitable upcoming discussion about our future. Inside my childhood yellow brick house, I had never experienced drama between my parents; I had no models for working out differences or making major life decisions with mutual respect in a way that brought people closer. I felt uneasy, and somewhat ill-equipped, about our next-steps discussion. My early social life had not aided the cause either.

I was brought up in Winnetka, Illinois, a place that felt socially isolating for a Jewish girl. There were few of us in grade school and still an insignificant number in New Trier High School, despite its enormous enrollment of 5,000, 1,200 of whom were in my graduating class. And while I had many non-Jewish friends, our family was excluded from their social gatherings, and I knew why. Many of the kids in the Winnetka community belonged to country clubs or lived in neighborhoods that were "restricted," a horrible euphemism for Jews Not Allowed. It gave me an early sense of compassion for other minorities.

As such, I bonded with our black maids and other service helpers. While they cleaned, cooked, and took care of me, my mother made them wear uniforms that embarrassed me. I refused to answer to "Miss Joan," insisting everyone call me "Joan" or "Joanie." I cringed when my mother, Dorothy, would ring her assortment of collectible bells for Lucinda to emerge from the kitchen and serve us dinner as though we were faux aristocracy. Sometimes, I hid the bells. My mother then installed a floor buzzer she could press with her feet. Some days I would throw a fit and run into the kitchen to eat dinner with Lucinda. My dad would tell my mom something like, "Do not make a scene." I would hear them arguing at the table, my brother quiet in the background. No matter. The staff was warm and accepting. I learned to cook with them, a rebellious expression of freedom insofar as my mom did not allow me in the kitchen because I would have made a mess when I was in there.

While I learned to fit in growing up, I often felt tentative about speaking up and standing my ground. Most of our nearby neighbors went to Sacred Heart, the local Catholic school, and so I barely knew them. I harbored huge crushes on the handsome dark-haired Irish boys with the deep blue eyes. At age fourteen, I decided that someday I would marry one. Years later, I fulfilled that dream when I met Irish boy Bill Barnes in college and we subsequently married. He had those Sacred Heart boy good looks and shoulders the size of the Brooklyn Bridge.

Midway through the day, I decided to spring a picnic surprise on Bill at the train station when he arrived from work. When he saw me from the train window, he beamed and his act of recognition caused my heart to skip a beat. We had a big hug on the platform before trotting off arm-in-arm.

Once in our Volkswagen bus, equipped with the picnic-style dinner I'd assembled, we drove the few miles to where our beloved sailboat was moored, north of Sing Sing. The smell of the old wooden boat was fresh, an unmistakable sign of the loving care we expended on it. We had often talked about what it would be like to have a boat on the water all year long, about abandoning harsh winters and living where things were happening: the sunny expanse of California, a place in the throes of incredible change, the country's cutting edge. We had dreamt of taking our prized boat, picking up our lives, and when it was time to start a family, starting that family in California. And now? Well, married now four years, the family had begun. This would be the next step in my youthful exploration, from teaching modern dance in various community centers to selling real estate and operating an antique business. I had little inkling what adventures would excite me once we arrived in California. I was willing to see what came my way.

I remember that the wind that evening was sublime and we talked dreamily of new beginnings. Much to my surprise and relief, the conversation flowed easily and a plan emerged: we would pitch caution to to the winds and go to California. We would trade our VW bus for a styling VW Westfalia camper equipped with a mini-fridge, sink, and pull-down bed. We would sell our possessions, camp across the country, and find jobs where we landed.

As we pulled on the jib and mainsail lines, we were engulfed in one of those magic moments between two people. We knew it, and we committed to the adventure ahead. We felt ourselves a family already, with two dogs and a baby in the offing. In virtually record time, we were ready to roll. We sold our little bungalow and antique inventory, packed up a few personal possessions, and hit the road.

As Bill and I navigated the amazing expanse of the United States, the excitement returned me to my camping exploits as a child, every summer at Camp Northland, nestled between Minnesota and Canada. Set on a primitive and pristine wilderness lake, the camp had no running water, only outhouses and saunas for weekly bathing. We washed our socks in the lake on wooden scrub boards. We arose at dawn to the sound of a gong and bunked down nightly to bugle-blown taps. In between, we cleaned our cabin for inspections worthy of drill-sergeant standards. It was all natural and effortless, this pioneering that, in later years, I saw as laying the essential groundwork of a budding entrepreneur. I found my grounding.

I believe we each have this "power place" in our core, and we know it when we find it, as we evolve through assessing and evaluating ourselves. Each time I sleep outside under the watchful eyes of the stars and ponder their mystery and feel the cold air kiss my face, I become, at once, all the ages I have been and no age in particular.

As Bill and I explored America, I thrived on simplicity and self-reliance. We grilled fried eggs, bacon, and hamburgers on a Coleman stove, slept in our VW camper, and enjoyed its cool extended-tent feature whenever the spirit moved us. Like the big colorful tent, I, too, felt expanded and vibrant. I was barefoot and braless and feeling my pregnancy. I wanted to live like that forever.

We arrived in California in late summer 1973 amid a time of radical change. Once planted on San Francisco terra firma, Bill landed a job at *The San Francisco Examiner*, thanks in part to a former *Time* colleague, Reg Murphy, whom the *Examiner* had recently hired as a publisher. For my part, I lacked a specific higher calling. While innately curious about countless things, no specific direction grabbed me, outside of my love of dance, where my limited talents left me shy of professional possibilities. This was all good, as I delighted in being pregnant and expectantly awaited the impending birth of our first child.

I enjoyed an ongoing love affair with my new home. The flower children with whom we mingled looked incurably happy, free, and on track to change the world. We had it all: our sweet innocence, the seeming invincibility of youth, and an abiding belief that we could change things. I felt sure-footed, ready to pursue our dreams of an idyllic life. San Francisco was the official heaven, beautiful and colorfully teeming with all kinds of people. Everywhere we looked, though, we saw more people who celebrated life. Berkeley, North Beach, Chinatown, Golden Gate Park, Marin County—all of it was right there. My backyard.

We made our home in an adorable vintage San Francisco flat and became parents. While not knowing exactly what to expect, my pregnancy buoyed me. I felt alive and full of energy the entire time, exhilarated and enthralled by the whole mysterious process. Having escaped most of the common difficulties of pregnancy, I was able to bask in the joy of life growing inside me. We went through natural childbirth—the absolute high of my life—with our first daughter, Meegan Dana. Talk about sobering: our daughter arrived and we were home less than 24 hours later, with no instruction manual and our families thousands of miles away, save for that first fleeting week, when my parents arrived from Chicago to bask in the birth of their granddaughter and provide loving assistance.

Once my parents left and the exhilarating rush of childbirth evaporated, the highs began to disappear and feelings of isolation moved in. I craved the company of other women who had chosen motherhood in the midst of the burgeoning Me Generation era, yet I felt anything but wedded to tradition. After all, Bill and I had come across the country to chart something apart. Plus, frankly, images of my own mom's frustrated existence flashed through my mind, and I knew I would need more than what the life of a full-time stay-at-home mom offered. I continued to dream about what pursuit might propel me to give it my all.

I was perfectly content to experiment, as I had before with a few disparate directions, each of which reminded me of how well I functioned with unstructured time and lots of heart. While not totally impatient, I was curious and excited about what my future would bring.

Bill was engaged with his career and I tried to conform to our new social environment, concerned about exposing my vulnerability. I longed to sort out my place and direction. I knew that without adult company and a suitable circumstance for my attention, my pangs of isolation and hunger for more purpose would increase exponentially. Mind you, things were not bad; I merely felt for the first time that uncompromising reality, "wherever you go, there you are."

Within a year, we moved across the Golden Gate Bridge to Mill Valley in Marin County to extricate ourselves from the incessant coastal fog. I joined a dance troupe that performed for children. We rehearsed often and my love of dancing reignited. I enjoyed the company and the inspiring choreography. As we practiced, Meegan sat smiling at me from her infant seat. Fellow dancer Karen Robbins and I became friends.

Then, an unanticipated opportunity appeared in my path. The Jewish Community Center (JCC) in Marin County offered Karen the job of directing its children's program. Karen hesitated because she was disinclined to undertake full-time work, as she had two small children. We put our heads together and devised a plan: a job share. Nothing short of revolutionary in 1974, our plan worked. The JCC hired us and we split the $10,000 salary.

Meegan settled in well to a part-time child care situation with a neighbor who took in several other toddlers.

My work at the JCC, while hitting the immediate spot, fell short of the passion that my core needed. I hungered for regular interaction with other new parents who had chosen, at least temporarily, the unfashionable traditional family life. I subsisted in a controlled state of restlessness. I yearned for an environment where women like me, with their infants and toddlers, could get together and enjoy their respective peers. Nothing of this sort existed. I was, however, about to stumble upon something major.

CHAPTER 3

∞∞∞∞∞∞∞∞∞∞∞∞∞∞∞∞∞∞∞∞∞∞∞

The Best Juju

OUR DEMARCATION OF RESPONSIBILITIES at the JCC job share was clear: Karen handled Jewish programming and I secular. Specifically, I ran the after-school classes for the kids and most of the family-oriented activities. I loved the purposeful work and the warm and caring community.

For the moment, I was grateful and content—and then, pregnant with my second child. So, while I daydreamed occasionally of a more passion-driven profession, a signature calling as it were, I had no gnawing urge for anything truly grand. I was content to bide my time until my bus happened by one day. My part-time job gave me some purpose and momentum while I focused on caring for baby Meegan, readying myself for baby number two, and nurturing the love I had for my husband.

On the other hand, I harbored deep concerns that life might devolve, locking me down with everything neatly arranged, much as my mom's life had been. This concern exhumed memories of the cellar in my childhood home, which for me rivaled Chicago's Field Museum of Natural History. Mom did not believe in junk drawers. She was a beauty, petite and naturally platinum blonde; people thought she resembled the film star Jane Powell. But she would putter around the cellar like a harried curator. Seeing her perched on that curvy chrome-legged stool with the plush pleather beige seat, as she meticulously parsed her discoveries, frightened the eight-year-old me. I marveled at her character-istically intense concentration, but shuddered that she reserved that sort of focus for organizing various-sized safety pins, rubber bands, matchbooks, and God knows what else. She was, to un-derstate, fussy; a more clinically accurate word would be com-pulsive. Her punctilious sense of arrangement was no idle hobby. To be sure, in a way, it involved her treatment of me, too—I was a neat projection of her sense of precision and beauty. As a child, I wished I could be loved without feeling I had to please for it. It felt like a rotten bargain against which I railed incessantly.

Despite these anxieties, my current life in California bore little resemblance to hers as a young mom. Yet, I wondered if I might still morph into her at some point. It could happen, I feared, despite the best of intentions. As my assemblage of new friends/sisters/confidants grew, I discovered that we each questioned our right to be our own woman, living our own real and differentiated lives. Conquering this expectation was no small feat. We were, in this time period, the first generation of women to bust out of conventional homemaker roles, even if just in small personal ways. While my inner conflicts marinated, I still felt comfortable as a mom within the cozy confines of my marriage.

Because any sense of creative challenge in my job at the JCC seemed unlikely to materialize, I knew I would likely not endure in this gig, however sweet. I held tight to the belief that the best juju derived from a spark, an ignition that leads to an idea, not the other way around. I bought in early to the belief that instinct trumps analysis, and to that end, when I got this physical sense, a confirmation in my body, like an acceptance letter, I was ready to act. We are called to action when an idea inhabits us as a virtual part of our cellular structure, I believe—when there is no choice. I like to think we are all artists for whom a pro-and-con chart about a proposed creative act is unimaginable prior to composing, painting, writing, creating . . . the work *must* be created. Nothing drives us like this kind of passion. But since no such passion had come my way, I was fine to sit tight. I could have gone out and sought opportunity, but that would involve another philosophy altogether. Presumably Howard Schultz, the leader who built Starbucks, shares a similar vision. In *Pour Your Heart Into It: How Starbucks Built a Company One Cup at a Time*, he mused: "I believe life is a series of near misses. A lot of what we ascribe to luck is not luck at all. It's seizing the day and accepting responsibility for your future. It's seeing what other people don't see. And pursuing that vision."

At the JCC, fortuity arrived wrapped in casual happenstance. As the particular significant week launched, it had all the earmarks of business as usual, and could have been a "near miss" of the kind Schultz described. I arrived one morning at the JCC and sauntered to the desk I shared partner-style with Karen in our nondescript portable trailer that housed the entire staff. The commotion and clutter gave the place the feel of a classic newsroom; everybody knew what everyone else was working on. It was old-school transparency.

That morning, JCC board member Carolyn Steinberg stopped by my desk to chat. She was an elegant thirty-something and had her two-year-old daughter, Aviva, in tow. I remember that the two were like something out of an ad, holding hands and dressed in pressed casual clothes. As they approached, the normal buzz in the trailer went silent. It was not every day that board members descended upon our modest offices. Naturally everyone was curious. After obligatory pleasantries, Carolyn exclaimed, "Joan, I am excited to tell you about the Kindergym class Aviva and I are about to go to at the Berkeley YMCA. We have been going a few weeks, but it is a good 45 minutes away. It might interest you; you're always looking at new programming. We are heading over in a few minutes."

With the mention of Kindergym, Aviva shouted gleefully "Kindergym" and actually jumped for joy. Her excitement was palpable. The look Carolyn gave her delighted daughter spoke volumes, and I perked up. While all parents light up when their kids display pleasure, this had a different quality. I was instantly curious and began to ask questions, and Carolyn upped the ante: "Come, come with us right now! Come see for yourself." The staff in the trailer were curious, too. As in a newsroom, everyone wanted me to go out, get the story, and report back. I was game.

Off we went across San Francisco Bay. I followed the two of them in my Volvo station wagon, so we would both be free to split up on the return trip. Driving over the bridge, passing San Quentin prison, and entering the East Bay, I would usually get lost in reverie about the infamous maximum-security prison resting ominously on its pristine real estate. I never wanted to take what I had in life for granted. That day, though, I fixated on something very different. Our destination had to hold something of great value. Why else would this affluent, well-connected woman drive virtually an hour each way across the East Bay to participate in this thing called Kindergym? While the new programming I had been able to find so far was largely unimpressive, I felt anticipatory as we neared Berkeley.

As we entered the YMCA, I sensed sheer pandemonium. Even to my nascent eye, the energy and ambiance overwhelmed, and I didn't know where to focus my attention. The kids were playing on the adult-sized gymnastic equipment that was also used by the University of California team: balance beam, pommel horse, parallel bars, trampoline, you name it. While hardly age-appropriate for toddlers—and potentially dangerous even with protective mommies looking on—I saw the value. I was a mom who would

treasure having fifteen or so other moms with similar-aged kids
to hang around with me. I noted the give and take of the moms
interacting, the skillful ways in which they assisted one another
with the kids during activities, and the spontaneous way their casual conversations led to after-class play dates.

There was more. A warm-hearted young man, who had been
circulating and cheering the kids on, brought out an army green
parachute near the end of the 45-minute session. His pied-piper
demeanor drew everyone together for some group play. I joined
the others, taking an edge of the parachute to billow it like a sheet.
As it flew up and down, the kids were enchanted. The braver toddlers went under and were hidden from view for a few seconds
until it rose back up. The more cautious toddlers watched from
the outside. Everyone was laughing. During the next game, the
children sat on the parachute while the adults walked around in
a circle, treating them to a ride. Whenever kids, for any reason,
opted out of the circle, everyone displayed warm acceptance and
a conspicuous lack of judgment for nonconformity. This was a
positive playground for kids with attentive, loving, and supportive adults attached to each child—mostly moms, with some dads
and a smattering of (presumably) nannies. Another group of parents and kids formed at the gym entrance for the next class. I felt
a surge of opportunity.

As I shivered in the cold, damp, and dark gym, an image of
what could be formed in my mind: a colorful, brightly lit room
filled with scaled-down play equipment sized for infants and
toddlers, kick-started with up-tempo music, and overseen by

an affirming teacher leading group activities around a multicolored parachute. I imagined the informality of this place and the smooth and spontaneous parental interactions that could happen there, where friendships could build and children could enjoy undivided attention and positive feedback. This, I realized, was what I needed for myself and Meegan. The thought that it might resonate with a broader community of moms was scintillating. I felt passion and purpose coalesce like a win-win green light.

My initial intuition quickly jumped to specifics. After I got back to Mill Valley, I ran my thoughts by Karen. She was supportive and enthusiastic and encouraged me to press on with the idea. I surveyed the available equipment in the marketplace and contracted a carpenter, Donny Becker, to ballpark potential costs and designs. Then, I considered marketing. I was sure there were many other moms nearby who, like me and Carolyn Steinberg, craved connection and community. I focused on how we might get media support for the idea, a natural tendency since I was married to a media guy and understood the power of press coverage. Who knew? If this was good, as I was starting to hope, local press might be all over it as a fresh story. Hell, it could be income producing—maybe even profitable! My first-line goal emerged: a unique service with enough cash flow to be self-supporting within a year. The JCC would be stoked, I knew, if I could make money doing this. Eventually, I came to understand that these were the musings of an entrepreneur.

Fundamental to my motivation was a powerful desire for community, a need to form genuine and thriving connections with other parents. This, I later realized, was another indication of entrepreneurial spirit: seeking the fulfillment of a personal need. When I was still living in New York, I'd had extensive experience participating in and leading consciousness-raising groups, primarily regarding pressing women's issues of the time. That experience had infused me with an "it takes a village" mentality; the social gatherings I envisioned had to be positive and upbeat. Everyone who took part should strive to drop their hardships and complaints at the doorstep. As still-new parents, we endured sleepless nights and many other challenges to our marriages. Many of us were underprepared for this life-altering transformation. The program I imagined would strive to amplify the *joys* of parenting. Let us celebrate how wonderful these magical young beings are, and how lucky we are to steward and enhance their development.

I sat down with Bill and inundated him with my stream-of-consciousness ideas. He listened with rapt attention and responded with queries that tested the idea—and me. The give-and-take was exhilarating. The more time we spent talking, the more excited I became. I tried to take a refined strategic approach. After devising a modest start-up plan, I approached the JCC board, which, lo and behold, authorized $3,000 to get the program started. I was thrilled, and while I had little insight into where this was headed, I had discovered that the whole effort hit a sweet spot for me: adventurous, entrepreneurial, a little risky, and for sure fun. Oh, yes, lest I forget—purposeful, too.

I bought as much equipment as I could find from catalogs, and then enlisted Donny Becker again to help design and build the new wooden Kindergym play equipment. With no budget for advertising, I had to get creative about finding exposure. I contacted the local county newspaper, the *Independent Journal*, about a story. The *IJ* was up for it and ran a full-page feature with color photos. That was the kind of public relations coverage no amount of advertising dollars could purchase. Things were falling into place. I had to trust my instinct that other moms (and some dads) shared the same powerful craving for community.

The next hurdle was finding the sort of dynamic and spirited teachers who would be critical to the success of the program. Where better to find them than among the JCC preschool teaching staff, convenient and homegrown? The commitment would be just a few extra hours a week. I was sure the preschool staff could use a little extra income, however modest. I knew most of them, and with the board's consent, I approached them, and hired a few.

The new Kindergym soared to life. As I had imagined that day in Berkeley, the JCC social hall was transformed. Adorned with a rainbow of vividly colored play equipment scaled to toddler size, a large color-blocked parachute for group play, songs, bubbles, and (before long) a "Gymbo the Clown" mascot, the room came alive with playful motion under the watchful eyes of compassionate, cheerful, and talented teachers, while we adults kibitzed and bonded. The budding vision materialized.

Within a few months the Kindergym program was a keeper. You could feel the formidable social power and sheer fun we had created. This was no summer fad, vulnerable to the whims of changing temperaments. Moms with Kindergym-age children passed through this time period in their life for a few years, and most (we learned) desired the same sense of community with others, and the same recreational opportunity for their little ones. The program had legs.

I've had plenty of chances to reflect on whether I created this opportunity or whether the business stork flew over and dropped it at my feet. Was it the product of some combination of synchronicity, desire, thoughtfulness, and being in the right place at the right time? These are my favorite kind of questions— they have no empirical answers. For sure, the "new" Kindergym did not arise from some grand business plan. While not total happenstance—I had what turned out to be a narrow, imperfect vision coupled with a percolating personal need—I also immediately sensed that these activities would fulfill a broader community need as well. I brought this program to life by taking advantage of the preexisting circumstances in which I had fortuitously found myself. So what did that mean?

One thing became clear: to succeed as entrepreneurs, we must *see* current circumstances not as they are but as what they can become. Often, our lives catapult from one point to another via a series of small choices that eventually morph into a broadly successful endeavor. As Peter Simms says in his insightful book *Little Bets*, a series of low-risk actions that explore new possibilities and build on each other can eventually lead to the development of a grand project, an end result that is not the product of a grandiose design or bold initiative. If we pay close enough attention to ourselves—our inner, not our outer selves—to what is happening around us, and to what we want to happen, we can identify new frontiers packed with fresh prospects. And when we align what we foresee with what moves us, we can accelerate the process of building something special.

Little did I know—and at the time, I knew very little—but my life was about to change in unimaginable ways.

CHAPTER 4

<small>∞∞∞∞∞∞∞∞∞∞∞∞∞∞∞∞∞∞∞∞</small>

Play Is Child's Work

BUZZING WITH FRESH ENERGY, the JCC was undergoing a veritable renaissance. The parking lot swarmed with moms, as the post–Kindergym class crowd was reluctant to give up the warmth and sisterhood of the communal company. This social dynamic awed me. Less than two weeks after we opened, one of our missions—creating connections among parents—was already happening. As women placed kids in car seats, I delighted in the kinds of conversational tidbits I overheard: "I'll call you." "OK, remember, lunch Friday, and bring your other son." "So great, thanks for including me. I will follow up. I look forward to it. Bye for now." And a chorus of, "See you at Kindergym next week!"

On a personal level, I was starting to discern a fine line between reaping the rewards of Kindergym for Meegan and me, and developing the program for the Center. I was building a business that, in part, I had hatched to satisfy a personal need. As I watched the parental parking-lot interplay with my head-of-program hat on, I felt a nagging concern that I not wind up like the "shoemaker's kid," watching all the moms make connections while I stayed isolated. Still, I realized that my initial interest in personal community could easily grow to embrace a broad, community-based program, which was exhilarating. While I did not realize it at the time, this was a flash-forward glimpse of the difficult life-work balance issues that would come down the pike.

Something had emerged in Kindergym that went beyond child's play. The enthusiasm was contagious and the groundswell of interest striking. The burgeoning participation numbers in the early days showed there had been a famine of connection and community. I gladly confessed to the comfort and validation I found in learning that I was not alone in my desire to find comrades in this new world of motherhood. I don't know exactly how I knew the program would be such a winner out of the gate, however small in the grand scale of things. I just did.

Despite the child-rearing implications of what we were doing, we made no claims that Kindergym offered a better this or that, which made it hard for child development or education experts to challenge the program's purpose or effectiveness—unless, of course, having fun was valueless. Dr. Burton White, author of *The First Three Years of Life*, would later say this about Gymboree:

"Children from four months on are really dedicated to the body, so, much of what [this program] offers makes sense. The presence of other parents sets up a support system." I continued to steer away from any claim that Kindergym (and later Gymboree) made a difference in terms of any aspect of child development. In those early days especially, I wanted to avoid the scrutinizing eyes of any researchers or analysts who purported to measure whether and to what extent preschool programs enhanced children's aptitudes and skills. The debate would get more extreme later on, especially when the "Super Baby" model debuted in the mid-1980s and parents began competitively tracking their children one school stage at a time to gain perceived future advantage for them, a cultural shift that downgraded fun as a factor in the preschool selection process. Dr. Benjamin Spock, author of the celebrated *Baby and Child Care*, said it best in the *New York Times* in January 1989, in commenting on the Super Baby Syndrome: "It's natural for parents in a country as competitive as ours to want to be sure that a child is keeping up with the crowd. . . . But I would want to make the point that children are learning very actively when they are playing, when they are following their own instincts."

That suited the Kindergym families fine. At Kindergym, our growing customer base seemed unconcerned with the scientific underpinnings of what the program entailed, as they continued to arrive in growing numbers. Fun trumped all! The moms made the ultimate consumer choice: coming week after week, and sometimes twice weekly. One anecdote I repeatedly heard warmed my heart. Participating moms often drove past our site

on *non*-Kindergym days, as at the time, the program still operated only a few days a week, in non-commercial, non-dedicated
spaces. As they drove by on their way elsewhere, their children
would clamor for Mom to divert to our parking lot for class. One
of my staff actually came up with suggested detour routes for
families to use on non-Kindergym days, so they could get to their
other destinations without having to deal with the fervent ap-
peals from their kids. The kids apparently wanted class *every* day.
How uplifting.

It didn't take long before we began to refine our programming. Each play program, while segmented by age, shared several traits. Each class was 45 minutes and had an adult (usually
a parent) accompany each child, while emphasizing an *exclusive*
focus on positive, upbeat, and fun play experiences. Even a casual
observer would notice that the bubbling energy in a Kindergym
class was anything but chaos. Children gravitated toward activities and equipment that thrilled them. I soon learned from Carolyn Mark, a JCC preschool professional and one of Kindergym's
first teachers, who later became part of the initial franchise community, that kids chose motor development challenges fundamental to their growth. That was my first clue that the defining
quality of the program was "play with a purpose," which would
become our long-standing tagline.

So, while fun and socialization for kids and parents alike
were from the get-go our core mission, and remained so, I came
to find out that Kindergym offered so much more. Specialists
working with special-needs children called me throughout the

first year or two, asking if they could mainstream their various populations into the classes, as the equipment was ideal for the many developmental challenges these children faced. Little did I know at the time that our play environment was inherently geared for more than "just" fun. It wasn't long before our news-letters could offer explanations as to what else was going on, besides the great joy of being together with other kids. Indeed, each piece of equipment had myriad uses, the purpose of which we explained in class and our newsletters. One child might want nothing more than to spin during what we called the ME time or "free exploration" part of class. This child would experience the unique perceptual question of whether she was moving or instead that "thing" next to her was moving. Another child might be sliding on a diminutive slide, integrating muscle coordination, touch, balance, and vision. Still another might want to crawl through a tunnel, helping neural pathways develop via cross-patterning and testing object permanence.

I came to understand, little by little, as the business grew and I brought in more child development teachers for the Kindergym program, that later academic learning was grounded in children first developing solid sensory systems built in sequential ways. The Kindergym environment, it turned out, was ideal for this kind of development, and it provided a place where the child's natural drive could be fulfilled. Mostly, Kindergym wanted par-ents to understand that this kind of play, which, as noted, we eventually characterized as "Play with a Purpose," helped chil-dren build positive self-regard while fostering solid parent-child connection. Mom or Dad would cheer on each child with hugs and consistent eye contact, affirming the whole experience.

In this nascent period, I was reserved about the parent-to-parent aspect of the Kindergym experience. As a marketer, I was uneasy about mentioning how Kindergym combated isolation, although as a "client" myself, I intuited—and later, research confirmed—that this dimension of the experience was vital to other parents and their decisions to enroll. No question, being together with your child in this positive place felt wonderful. Equally rewarding, however, was the opportunity for companionship with other parents. With friendships forming organically this way, and helping to diminish the isolation so many new parents feel, Kindergym became something of a home away from home for many. Much like the Starbucks store model, which was designed to encourage people to congregate in places other than home or work, our adults felt "at home" in Kindergym. How could we pollinate this dynamism more widely, and share this experience with a larger community?

With a little more than one year under my belt with the Kindergym program, I suggested to the JCC board that we open a second Kindergym in Mill Valley, my hometown. Impressed with the early enrollment numbers and the financial success we were having with the program, the board approved. And off I went, taking another small step to see what the unknown would bring.

In the words of tech guru Alan Kay, "The best way to predict the future is to invent it." The second location, opened a few months after I got board approval, replicated the original site's enrollment numbers, and I delighted in watching children and adults march into the new Kindergym, a pilgrimage of jubilant new believers. Almost from the start, both facilities turned a profit, which fueled support for the JCC charitable programs and spread the good feelings around the larger table. These were modest beginnings, for sure, but they made me proud and abated the internal restlessness I'd felt when we first came to California.

My marriage was strong and there was, more or less, balance between family life and building Kindergym at the JCC. This was a sweet and simple time of my life. The scale of things in my world was still relatively easy to grasp. While this was not a "stop time forever" moment, this period was quite worthy, I think, of a freeze frame. You know, one of those easy intervals in each of our stories that deserve a pause. This chapter of my life began to fill a personal void that had received no attention since I came to California—basking in innovative activity—adding to the richness of life as woman, a mom, a wife, and a professional.

Such balance and simplicity, however, can fall prey to the temptations of more. As my contentment found a pleasant level, Max Shapiro, the JCC president, made it clear to me he thought Kindergym held commercial potential beyond the JCC. Max was an entrepreneur who had recently sold his interest in basketball camps he operated with basketball legends John Wooden and Rick Barry, and he was looking for a new business opportunity. He was sharp and savvy, so I paid attention. Max had a modest proposal. He wanted to partner with me to grow Kindergym into a small business. He offered to stake $3,000 as a passive investor, in exchange for which I would build the business in a 50/50 deal.

Now, freeze on that moment. At the time, I had no such plan of my own. I was happy and satisfied with what I had put together with the JCC. All was good, was it not? But as I've learned, that is not how an entrepreneur thinks. We are more like kids in a candy store: incurably optimistic, inclined to suppress caution and doubt in the belief that we can make real our ever-redefining vision. Taking risk and looking beyond barriers is a necessary ingredient for business success.

So when Max approached me with this simple notion, he triggered something in me that had been lying in wait. My instincts recoiled at the prospect of responding, "I am good, no thanks." Rather, I figured I was a mere 28 years old. What did I have to lose? Looking back, I realize "bring it on" was probably a truer characterization of my excitement at the prospect of becoming even more engaged with Kindergym. So I made the deal, and in 1976, Max and I opened the first commercial Kindergym site in San Mateo at Peninsula Temple Beth-El, whose managers I convinced to allow us use of their social hall a few days a week. Incredibly, our very first group of classes made us profitable. The success was in part thanks to more supportive media, this time from the *San Mateo Times*, which ran a beautiful feature story much like the one the *Independent Journal* had run a few years earlier.

Six months later, the partnership opened a second location in San Jose. It too did well. Whoa. Hiring qualified teachers who could install a business telephone line in their home and operate

Kindergym as both teacher and administrator was far easier than I had imagined. The local papers (very pre-Craigslist) yielded an abundance of talented candidates, and I chose my first two manager-teachers. Both had teaching backgrounds and the signature positivity and high energy I was looking for. They were stoked to take part in the business aspect as well, and felt ownership over the program in their communities.

We were becoming a local media darling that some called a "pre-preschool phenomenon." By the time 1977 started, I could not have been more pleased. My life was quite full. Professionally, I had two thriving commercial locations and the JCC job share; Meegan was three and sister Cecily almost eighteen months; and Bill and I were flourishing. Balance, well, it came and went. Suffice it to say, we were managing just fine.

There were, however, barely discernible indicators of rougher roads ahead. No matter how well things were going, from time to time, when I felt inundated, my internal self-confidence went lax and my spirits sagged. This was nothing new. It had always been my personality to take on a lot and see limits only when I became overwhelmed. Now, though, little telltale signs of dissonance began to emerge, more intense than before. These did not seem serious, and were definitely not debilitating—except that my early childhood training to cover up any sort of insecurity compounded the problem. I began longing to rid myself of the fear of exposure. I was worried that if anyone learned of my self-doubt, it would make me seem "less than," or worse yet—unlovable. My impulse to bury these passing anxieties and refuse to acknowledge them was powerful. I was uncertain, though, where I might find a release valve for the mounting pressure.

This harked back to my early childhood. My mom would light up when her canasta club ladies would kvell over my curly red hair or rosy coloring. Looks were a trump card in this group. Hearing, "She's a beauty, Dorothy" was the equivalent of a victorious sweep on card-playing day. But rather than feeling she was my ally or champion (let alone my mom), I felt more like she was someone from whom I was trying to negotiate good treatment. The best course was to follow the rules and always try to add extra sprinkles of charm for insurance. I would often retreat from the effort to secure love from my mother and stow away my feelings, along with my own collection of little trinkets—mostly gifts my dad brought me whenever I was sick and had to stay in bed, each a tiny emblem of love. We would eat dinner together on trays in my bedroom and then ceremoniously deposit the new gift in the cigar box where I kept them, a ritual of profound pleasure. I secreted it away in my closet, behind the shoe rack.

For as long as I could remember, I had chased patience—oxymoronic as that sounds—and hoped to make my mother my friend. I wanted to feel calm, a sense of internal well-being, which I knew I was supposed to feel, what with all the good stuff my life held. But a small crack started to open inside me.

As Kindergym percolated with success, I sometimes reveled in memories of time I spent at Camp Northland, my beloved childhood sleepaway camp, where I always felt it easiest to be me—a counterpoint to always being "on" at home. There was no judgment, no pressure, no expectations. Like Camp Northland, Kindergym provided me with the judgment-and-pressure-free environment I had lacked as a child. As a budding entrepreneur, I was starting to express more of my innate love of adventure, as well as my aptitudes for resilience, problem solving, and risk tolerance. What portion of these abilities came packaged in genetic makeup, and what portion had developed otherwise? Is knowing yourself the highest form of entrepreneurial acumen? How else do we face and conquer frontiers?

I was aware that transforming Kindergym to a commercial model was an entirely different experience. I knew that getting involved with this would put my sense of personal identity and worth on the line. The business escalation would compel me through a maze of fears and test my core mettle. This was the ultimate gamble. I had no business background or training. I had no great, majestic plan. Regardless, I could see this was not a time for retreating to personal comfort zones. Fears and doubts notwithstanding, my confidence was growing when it came to running this modest business, and I was beginning to sense its possibilities. At least at its current scale, I thought I could be all things at all times for this project. Once I turned the commercial corner, though, success would require an open-field jaunt through prospective failure. Risk all, gain all? I was there, ready or not. My instincts screamed act, and so act I did.

Kindergym's success to that point derived 100 percent from my labors, since Max, a passive investor, was on the sideline. I had a bold thought. Why not take the bull by the horns? With the support and encouragement of Bill, I asked Max if he was willing to be bought out at double his investment. He agreed, and I acquired his half of the business for $6,000, which I financed through a second mortgage on our family home. I now had designs on expansion. *Scratch that itch.*

Once the business's profits were consistent, and fortified by my confidence that I now had a business with real growth potential in my grasp, I left my JCC job share and continued to expand. The ensuing draught of pure entrepreneurial spirit intoxicated me. I had a replicable format that was driven entirely by public relations, with little paid-advertising cost. In those days, we guerilla marketed using low-cost, unconventional means, through things like well-viewed community bulletin boards and various printed newsletters. Best of all, great word of mouth and press coverage sustained us.

In the proverbial blink of an eye—that is how it seemed at the time—Kindergym became a growing force. By 1979, three years after establishing the initial commercial site, I had nine Kindergyms operating from south San Francisco to the budding Silicon Valley. These were not permanent commercial locations. Rather, each was set up a few days per week in a church or temple hall. We had to remove the equipment each day, or every few days, to allow the facility use of the space for other purposes. We stored the equipment in portable sheds or random nooks and crannies on the site. We then schlepped the equipment back into the play space the next scheduled day.

Kindergym thrived in San Mateo and Santa Clara counties,

30-45 miles from our home in Mill Valley. Administratively, I had outgrown the garden shed in the backyard of our home and leased a modest office in Burlingame, near the San Francisco airport, to be closer to operations. There was something symbolic in having a dedicated leased office.

Now, as Kindergym prospered, I saw my life becoming different than that of the other moms I knew. Most, if not all, were more traditional stay-at-home moms or were perhaps part-time schoolteachers, nurses, or employed in some other sector where women had historical acceptance. I was no anomaly—not yet anyway. Still, no one else I knew was an entrepreneur and growing a business. I was proud: my little business sprouted from scratch was profitable, grossing about $250,000 annually.

The growth of the business had a cascading feel to it, and the ripples of internal doubt I experienced continued to shake my footing. I was often curious, while not particularly cautious: *Where am I headed? How will I manage wherever it goes?* Fear, while contained, began to bloom.

CHAPTER 5

∞∞∞∞∞∞∞∞∞∞∞∞∞∞∞∞∞∞∞

The Entrepreneurial Compass is Set at Instinct

I MEANT IT WHEN I SAID I had no grand plan. Search as you might, you would have found no entrepreneurial crystal ball on my desk or, for that matter, any how-to business literature. This was on-the-job training. I think the most important tool in the entrepreneurial toolbox may well be an instrument that mimics a crystal ball. Call it a confluence of instincts and intuition that form into a foggy vision that excites you. Imagine my surprise, therefore, when in 1979, as Kindergym was becoming a community darling, the Stanford Graduate Business School Alumni Association invited me to speak to B-school aspiring entrepreneurs. At the time, Chuck Bernstein, the brother of my best friend Carolyn André (who later would become instrumental in various marketing initiatives for

Gymboree while working as senior VP of marketing at advertising giant Batten Barton Durstine & Osborn, aka BBDO) was the head of the Alumni Association and its programming. Chuck was excited to bring in a local successful entrepreneur, operating in Stanford's backyard, to talk about the nuts and bolts of building a business from the ground up.

This invitation was the ultimate irony, considering that I would have failed most (OK, likely all) B-school classes at Stanford if I had been an enrolled student. Too bad there were no classes offered that covered "winging it on a whim." How do you deliver lessons in chutzpah?

I am not sure you can teach entrepreneurial instincts anymore than you can teach someone with a tin ear to be a chanteuse. But I was catching on, using whatever nonlinear methods I had at my disposal, and as I did, my confidence built steadily.

The organic expansion of Kindergym suited my sense of the best way for us to grow—free-form atop a strong, underlying sense of order. To some extent we had blinders on, like thoroughbreds, as I insisted we press onward, not yielding to the distractions posed by competitors and imitators. Unlike many who felt it important to stay ahead of the competition—whatever that means—I implored my colleagues not to succumb to trends emerging in other parent classes. How far this approach could take us was unclear at the time, as market realities always have a way of intruding, but for the moment I felt this benchmark kept us true to our purpose and kept us from peering over our shoulders.

Despite the temptation to become swollen-headed with our

adoring press, I felt we mostly stood clear of becoming too enamored with ourselves. I tended to see the world as I hoped it could be, which I felt helped me with risk-taking and innovation. I endeavored to mimic the toddlers at Kindergym themselves, especially when it came to testing new limits. Working collaboratively, our company's culture was reminiscent of a functional family. Maybe it was no surprise that while speaking at Stanford in my "professorial" debut, the students responded well to my unorthodox lecture, which challenged them to imagine and chart a course that felt intrinsically right for them, especially in terms of the early stages of building a business and giving life to their vision.

This freedom to act from the gut, I would learn eventually, was not some undisciplined or reckless management style. Some decades later, as I educated myself in business through reading and attending presentations, I learned that despite B-school conventional wisdom, most important business decisions made by well-respected leaders are derived from or shaped by instinct. This suggests that we ultimately feel most comfortable going with what we "feel" rather than what we "know."

Despite my childhood imperatives to figure out *why* something was important rather than having the green light to just *want* something because it felt right, I felt free to act from my most authentic place. With this came confidence that had eluded me growing up. This is not to say that feelings of "not as good as" or "am I worthy" got deep-sixed—hardly. These worries stuck and tended to surface when triggered. Mostly, I acted with assuredness from instinct, backed up by some data of course, while a small insecure voice eked out kernels of doubt. Now it is my practice to monitor these internal dynamics, but at the time I had little understanding of how this dichotomy worked effectively.

From 30,000 feet, I continued to find my way and, so far, things were working out. My nine commercial sites remained housed in San Mateo and Santa Clara counties. I operated in those remote areas because I didn't want to compete with the JCC, and our growth continued that way. Plus, the markets in those venues were strong and showed no sign of weakening, an operational comfort zone.

On the home front, my daughters were happy in our old-fashioned neighborhood. Our lively village was a beautiful mix of people. We lived next door to a famed local soccer coach and folk singer, and across the street from a firefighter. On any given day at the local Sweetwater Saloon, a thriving music venue, locals like Huey Lewis, Bob Weir, Grace Slick, Bonnie Raitt, or Carlos Santana might take the stage as a cameo for fun. Later, brilliant performers like Dana Carvey and the late Robin Williams would do likewise at the Throckmorton, the local live theater. It would be a long time before Mill Valley's real estate market surged and pushed out the middle of the bell curve. My children loved the freedom to trot through the neighborhood on foot, bike all over, or even head into town unescorted. It was the last of times when, as parents, we felt safe having our kids wander the village streets. Those were sweet growing-up years.

Bill was working as the political editor of the *San Francisco Examiner,* covering breaking national stories of the day, like the hideous Jim Jones and Peoples Temple tragedy. When the Jonestown mass suicide occurred and law enforcement raided Jones's San Francisco headquarters, we learned that Bill's name was on a hit list that Jones maintained for assumed enemies he might want to avenge at some point. Bill also cracked a story about illegal massage parlors that exploited underage girls who were enticed to leave Asia with the ruse of a fresh start as a masseuse, only to be conscripted for prostitution. He was also one of the first journalists that Dianne Feinstein, then the acting mayor of San Francisco, and later a U.S. senator, called prior to her national TV announcement of the tragic murders of Mayor George Moscone and City Supervisor Harvey Milk. Bill was in the center of the action and understandably full of pride about his work.

While we had a wonderful Scottish au pair, Brenda, I was going full-throttle in all-encompassing mom-mode. The balancing act of mom, wife, and business builder, not to mention my efforts to have strong friendships and a healthy lifestyle, grew more difficult each day. While today the "balancing act" is a cliché discussed everywhere moms congregate, in the late 1970s, it was hardly the norm. We working mothers were inventing ourselves among the majority of stay-at-home moms and the smattering of women in part-time roles as teachers and nurses.

While my life appeared to be in balance, the fullness of the days began to trigger stress and drain my energy. I began eating more, and then finding different ways to offset the caloric intake. While diet pills and amphetamines were not strangers to me—I had been using these since high school, and they had fed my quiet obsession with appearing thin—I found myself taking a few extra now and again. Other subtle, barely perceptible signs of anxiety started to occur. I began to pay even more attention to the scale. I sometimes worried about my ability to control my eating. I occasionally felt down after eating—nothing major, more like a wave of mental fatigue. None of these behaviors produced regular concerns; they were random, and resided quietly in the back of my consciousness. For sure, there was no panic—but in hindsight, a foundation of trouble was being laid.

I was in a quandary about the business's growth. Various internal voices clamored for different options. One voice argued for no change, which would allow me to stay somewhat in step with other moms I knew. If I opted for a no-growth mode, maybe I could keep everything afloat and stay comfortably close to the middle ground. Growth would drag me further away from any mom-norm of the day, entailing a personal paradigm shift. Another very loud voice wanted to grow the community of play centers. That felt so right. To not grow would mean an artificial stop to what I was building. The most pragmatic voice put forward this point of view: something would have to give, or I would dive-bomb sooner rather than later.

Despite the cautionary voices, I felt compelled to build. I felt no stop in me. If a crash and burn was on the horizon, well, I would hopefully either deflect or deal. In the present circumstances, I still had too much go in the tank. Whatever sacrifices I needed to make I assumed would be worth the cost and effort. I could not fathom a satisfying way to leave or cut back the business, even if it meant I might stumble or be harmed in the process.

In fairness, this was all uninformed musing. I had no idea how this would or could play out in real time. In such circumstances, we rarely do. In any event, at this juncture, I consigned my internal naysayers to solitary confinement and brooked no more discussion. Lockdown for them! I went all in, and poised for more.

I did know, regardless, that I needed pressure relief. I offered partnerships to my main manager-teachers, Ann Johnston at the San Mateo play center and Harli Rabow in San Jose. Both were up for it. This allowed me to transfer to their shoulders my major long-distance daily operational headaches, which included spontaneous road trips at 7:00 a.m. to haul heavy play equipment out of storage because the set-up guy could not get there for some reason. Moving beyond a sole-proprietorship model had obvious upsides. Sharing equity with Ann and Harli was well worth it for the decrease in pressure alone. Soon after Ann and Harli geared up in their new roles, I saw how good a move it had been. They were talented and dedicated. The personal, internal compromise this new arrangement required of me seemed healthy and wise.

A few months after I partnered with Ann and Harli, Bill landed a once-in-a-lifetime opportunity: the *Examiner* assigned him to cover the first 100 days of the Reagan administration in Washington, D.C., from January to March of 1980, and he negotiated an all-expenses-paid trip for the family to join him! This was a unique career break for Bill, even though it meant I had to commute to and fro for midweek trips to oversee the business. My partnership arrangement with Ann and Harli proved serendipitous.

We arrived to greet the D.C. winter, with its chilly, gray-skied environs, and as jowly, gray-suited men marched about the lettered streets of the nation's capital and flexed their presumed power muscles, we got comfortable in our provisional home. Freed from our routine life, our family bond strengthened as we navigated this adventure. This D.C. getaway was forevermore mythic in our family folklore. The togetherness deepened our family connection.

Predictably, when we returned from D.C., so did routine life. Little was routine or predictable, however, about business. Out of the blue, or so it seemed, various women approached me about starting their own Kindergym. Could they buy a franchise? *A franchise?* I knew next to nothing about this business model, except that it seemed a little company called McDonald's operated in this fashion with grand success. This was uncharted territory for me, fraught with potential failure on all fronts. I took a hard right turn from my characteristic wing-it propensity, however, and sought top-shelf advice.

I reached out to George Gaber, a dear family friend I had known since early childhood. A wise man, George was the marketing director at Jim Beam responsible for those classic collectible bottles. George referred me to Bud Jacob, who, George extolled, possessed extensive background in franchising and was the ideal person with whom to vet this concept. Bud Jacob had been part of the start team with one of the franchise industry's granddaddies, Midas, and later moved to Arby's, working both for the parent company and as an owner of several Arby's restaurants in California and Chicago.

Bud and I enjoyed an instant connection, the kind where you feel you have known someone for years. It turned out that he, like George, knew my family from Chicago. He liked what I showed him about the business. From his vantage point, Kindergym was ripe for franchise development. He emphasized many positive aspects of the business opportunity, including the low capital outlay and the unique entry niche for women, especially to operate as a part-time business out of the home. Bud also warned me about franchise system challenges. He pointed out the potential stresses between the franchise business and the existing play centers. At the macro level, a conflict could arise between, on the one hand, the ever-present need to innovate, improve, and market the play centers; run first-rate model corporate centers; and pursue solid corporate profits; and, on the other hand, the commitment to train and build support for a strong, profitable, expanding franchise community. I felt confident I could manage this dichotomy, although I did not know how. I presumed I would figure out how to address and solve conflicts as they arose.

I was fired up. My dream of a community of like-minded women who combined professional and family focus was taking shape. The idea of a replicable hometown business that offered core community value, where individual women leaders could bring their personal pride and touches to a business, seemed like an unmatchable opportunity. What's more, I felt capable of leading this effort. I cruised ahead with labor-intensive applications to the Federal Trade Commission for the required approvals to become a bone fide franchisor, and within several weeks, "Kindergym, doing business as Joan Barnes," was a licensed franchise. I approached Ann and Harli to see if they would convert their partnership to franchise ownership. Ann was willing and we made the deal, and she became the proud owner of the San Francisco market. Harli was unwilling. After a tussle, I borrowed money from my father to buy her out. I was reluctant to ask him, mindful of his tight financial resources, but I was brimming with confidence about the business prospects. And, to back up his own vision of those prospects, Bud himself produced an early Kindergym franchisee: his wife, Lois, who bought the San Francisco East Bay territory, which covered Berkeley through Hayward (and which would grow to five locations).

Still, I was anxious about going further in this direction. Money was tight. How could we develop a franchise program without disposable capital? I lacked the resources needed to market a real franchise program. I learned, however, that I did not need much at this juncture. Insiders and word-of-mouth interest began to bring people to me! Each new center begot the next and the next, populating our community. Blessed was I. Before long, we had eight franchise locations to complement our nine play facilities. The Zees, as we affectionately called our franchisees, were off to a good start, and we had the beginnings of a replicable system. I was busting with excitement. The economics were shiny: each franchisee was profitable early on, and our corporate sites were also in the black.

Then, this jolly train hit a bump on the tracks, a setback I experienced as a monster problem. The United States Patent and Trademark Office (USPTO) rejected my trademark application for "Kindergym." The USPTO deemed the name "generic." Perhaps this explained why I, acting naively and without a second thought, had heard no protest when I copied the name from the Berkeley program I had visited years ago, which had inspired the business in the first place. Regardless, I was deflated. Kindergym had brand recognition, derived from five years of operational experience, and we had grounded franchise loyalty in the name. How was Kindergym generic? Did that mean we were done? How was I, as founder and leader, supposed to respond? Was I resilient enough to craft a solution? After all, any franchise's bedrock is its name and the franchisor's ability to protect that name. Without that, there might be no sustainable franchise business.

This was my first major business call to arms, testing my ability to hold up in the face of setback. I needed a new name for the business, and fast! We hunkered down and focused intensely on trying to come up with something that felt right. Bill and I spent countless hours rummaging for a substitute. Every day, we exchanged endless thoughts—and sometimes playful barbs—during our regular hikes or bike rides. Pieces of paper were strewn throughout the kitchen of our house (kitchens must be the universal birthplace of deep thinking). While the fear of failure had me circling my psychic wagons, I had fun collaborating with Bill this way, and his steadfast loyalty and willingness to hang tough and be supportive calmed me. We shot each other's ideas down with no judgment or defensiveness. While this was my business, I counted on him for creative brainstorming and a loyal ear. He was damn smart.

Despite the fun we had with it, no new name grabbed me. We couldn't figure this one out. After three weeks, my concern turned to worry. The joy of the process no longer propped me up. The temptation to settle for mediocre escalated. Time was closing in.

Then, while jogging, Bill had an epiphany. As soon as he was able, he found a pay phone and called me. When I answered, I heard a breathless Bill huffing and puffing, and then the words: "Gymboree, Gymboree." *Yes!*

I loved it. We could scrap the endless names we'd recorded on whatever paper was handy, assembled haphazardly in an apple basket on the kitchen table. "Gymboree" immediately sounded so perfect. It embodied the spirit of what I had built. Much to my pleasure, the name received uniform goodwill during our informal test among people we knew, our threshold "mother-in-law" market research. Knowing we had to get it right, however, we had our advertising agency (BBDO and my friend Carolyn) conduct mall-intercept interviews and other research to confirm our expectation that "Gymboree" generated the right good vibe in the public arena. The research showed that parents found the name upbeat and knew implicitly it concerned children. We chose a top-notch trademark firm to conduct diligence and fast-track the legal process. The USPTO, this time, got out of the way. Gymboree got the approval it deserved within a few weeks.

The franchise system launch and the name snafu were powerful experiences that steeled me for future predicaments. They taught me early-stage lessons about the complexity of management teams. It seemed natural to bring on people whose gifts and talents far exceeded mine, and it was important to know that the company's success—and mine as a by-product—sprang from bringing on the best people. I was neither intimidated nor concerned that others would outshine me. The company was the grand reflection of all its superstars building the energy from within. As CEO, my essential talent had to be picking the members of the orchestra, inspiring them to play, and rewarding their considerable talents. Micromanaging did not interest me. I preferred the role of conductor, and was stirred to identify the needed virtuosos, so that we could single out candidates who fit the Gymboree culture and nurture their talents. I began to see that my leadership gifts were most critical to our organization in my role as "inspiritrix."

The market transition from one brand name to another was textbook. There was no backlash, hiccup, or problem of any sort. In addition to lessons in management, I learned that patience and stick-to-itiveness can help make a silk purse resolution out of a sow's ear problem. What had seemed like a major setback transformed into an opportunity. We had a better, more suitable name that sang, and we were rolling. I felt on top of the world. Adios, "Kindergym." It was real. Welcome "Gymboree." We shall steward you well. And off we went.

CHAPTER 6

∞∞∞∞∞∞∞∞∞∞∞∞∞∞∞∞∞∞∞∞∞

Meet Luck, Your Friend

LUCK, AS I LEARNED, is a big part of entrepreneurial success, so much so that it often seems prerequisite. As when playing Texas hold 'em, when you accept a blind bet and raise the stakes, you count on Lady Luck. As the expression goes: "I see and raise you." That's the daring component of working with presumed luck on your side. Luck-spawned opportunities sprout constantly, often unexpectedly. It is not enough, however, to detect the lucky moment, for luck only *opens* doors. It is decisive action that trumps all. Indeed, some say the real genius in entrepreneurial triumph lies in both recognizing and taking advantage of the gift when it arrives. I'm not sure about the genius part, frankly, but you'll see what I mean about finding gifts of opportunity at the door.

While at the Gymboree offices one morning in 1980, I experienced a first: a mom (Alice) wanted to have a meeting with me. Ann Johnston, the San Francisco franchisee who had converted her partnership interest to a franchise business, assured me that Alice came without any kind of alarming agenda. Despite the rest-at-ease assurances from Ann, I was cautious and anticipatory.

After introducing us, Ann left to allow us to speak privately. I first learned that Alice and her two children had been regular Gymboree participants for over two years. Then, she said, "Joan, I adore what Gymboree stands for and what my kids and I have gotten from the program. I can't tell you how much the kids and I look forward to weekly classes. I have made many friends there that I know will be lifelong. This program is nothing short of revolutionary. I and so many others thank you."

Spontaneously, she reached for my hand with both of hers across the small conference room table that separated us. She followed with a squeeze and a smile, full of sincerity. I returned a nod and a grin, awaiting the real agenda. Then she revealed the lead: "I have a dream to own a Gymboree operation."

She looked to me for cues. Lightly, I pulled my hand away, clasping both in front of me. I leaned forward to convey interest, politely, as I knew we had saturated the Bay Area markets.

"Joan, my husband, Richard, and I both are really excited about the idea of buying a franchise and growing with Gymboree. We know there aren't any local franchises available and we are willing to relocate outside the Bay Area. Is this something you would consider?"

I flashed a full-hearted smile and sat quietly with her for a moment. Her palms now rested flat on the table. I replied, "Alice, for starters, I am so touched by how much Gymboree has impacted you and most appreciative of the homework you have done. And more to the point of our get-together, I'm delighted to hear of your interest."

Before I could continue, she again placed her hand on mine as if to say, one more thing, and added: "I must mention I'm in contact with other moms, and I'm confident they would be willing to be franchise candidates outside the area, if the company is so inclined. I guess I am the appointed ombudswoman, if you will."

Her smile oozed natural charm. I felt myself nod again as if we had a routine going. We chatted some more. I told her I would consider her request and review whether it could possibly fit into our plans. We hugged as we departed.

My ride home was a blur. For some reason, I was flooded with vivid memories of when Bill and I traipsed across the nation to start our new life in California. I imagined aspiring moms chasing similar adventures with a similar zeal to expand their lives. I foresaw our small Bay Area franchise community of like-minded moms, which combined their family focus and their professional ambitions, turning into a national business model that minimized start-up pressure and risk of failure. (At the time I knew nothing of the research I learned about years later, including reports in *Inc.* magazine in 2011 and 2012, which showed that our specific Gymboree franchise model had a relatively low failure rate compared with venture-backed start-ups.)

Lady Luck had laid an expansion opportunity at my feet. The meeting with Alice fueled visions of an expansive franchise market well beyond our current operational borders. The prospective new direction was exciting—and scary. A pattern had emerged. I would settle on a new operational reality, business would become good and comfortable, and then a tempting new opportunity would arise. Our Bay Area boutique operations, once a reach, were now quite manageable, my arms fitting snugly around them. The new fork in the road tantalized me, and I wrestled introspectively with questions about my capacity: *Is this in my best interest? Does bigger mean more successful? Will constant growth zap my core drive and enthusiasm? Will I take myself too seriously or, conversely, become complacent? Will I—ugh—fail? Are these kinds of doubts healthy?*

While my worries were real, I kept them to myself, cramming them deeper into my internal world and hoping they would either go away or sort themselves out. I was concerned about feeling diminished if others knew about my insecurities. As a result, I always tried to project self-assuredness. But in doing so I denied myself an outlet and disregarded my mounting stress. I had no real measure by which to determine if my feelings were extreme. I assumed that few entrepreneurs felt the doubts that I did, and that confidence would replace these pesky demons if and when new challenges manifested in results.

At home later that afternoon, with the girls still in school and Bill at the newspaper, I puttered about the house considering the possibilities. Physical movement stimulated my thinking in ways that otherwise might remain stifled if I were planted at a desk. I felt titillated by the possibilities of greater expansion. It was relatively easy to acknowledge, considering how I'd sought and found help earlier, that it was essential to have seasoned expertise if I went this route. Specifically, I needed a major in-house franchise expert and a well-conceived growth plan. This would be a major play.

The next day, I sprang into action. I approached Bud Jacob again. I proposed that he leave Arby's and join Gymboree to spearhead a national franchise rollout. After all, he had witnessed firsthand his wife's success as a franchisee the past few years. Moreover, he was an excellent fit with our women-dominated culture, and he was as experienced as they came in the industry. Bud was enthusiastic and needed six months to extricate himself from his current relationship. Further, Bud and George Gaber also knew a venture capitalist named Stuart Moldaw at U.S. Venture Partners (USVP), and suggested Stuart might be primed to finance our growth, especially insofar as USVP was at the time starting the first-ever consumer venture fund. If Gymboree could be included, imagine.

Pause here for a moment of caution. George wanted a heart-to-heart with me before I met Stuart. He implored me to think carefully about what might follow if USVP became my venture capitalist. He knew me well, including my tendency to leap without restraint. He minced no words. He explained that venture capital money would likely put me on an irreversible path that would have a huge impact on me personally, including what I held most dear—my children, marriage, and close friends. He reminded me of how much I relished spontaneity, and made it clear that the scrupulous eyes and timetables of the venture capitalists would cost me that kind of freedom. He underscored that I would be laboring under chronic pressure to satisfy the financial expectations of investors, which could lay waste to any wishes to live as I might otherwise choose. While VCs might be proud of the business, might extol the leader's virtues and display other signs of humanity, they were in it for the money and would expect me to do whatever was necessary to deliver the goods, and not always what I might feel was necessary. For them, the bottom line was, well, the bottom line. I thanked George profusely for this unvarnished caveat emptor.

His warnings triggered the various internal concerns I'd been pondering all along. I reviewed the various risks again. Like a congregation member does with her rabbi, I was to spend a few hours with George virtually every week for years to come. He was a close friend, part father and part counselor, and he made me laugh like no one else. It is not every day we can claim someone in our life who influences us so profoundly. In Jewish culture, it's common to say we live on in the hearts and minds of those who follow. While I made no claim to the kind of wisdom possessed by George Gaber, I was trying to live in a way that touched souls and left imprints that would last long past my own life. Would this be possible if I sought venture capital funding to fuel Gymboree's expansion? Some entrepreneurs may know this kind of thing going in; I was still learning on the job.

A regular visit from my parents coincided with this decisional crossroads about Gymboree's potential growth funding. Mom's feelings seemed mixed about my success. She kvelled to her friends about how her daughter had created a popular and successful business, but when we were together, she cross-examined me about how my time away affected her grandchildren. Dad was characteristically supportive. Not inherently ambitious himself, he wanted to be sure I did not get in over my head. He lovingly suggested that I consider leaving well enough alone. His concern was genuine. I felt no pressure of any kind from him. Thinking back, Dad knew me inside out, including my propensity for biting off too much and becoming overwhelmed. He was alerting me to the need to understand myself better. As I had with George, I thanked him for his concern, and, in words that reverberate to this day, he replied, "Honey, whatever makes you happy."

Often I think parents know us better than we can imagine, or are willing to concede. Embracing advice when tough life moments present us with big decisions can be difficult enough, but when the sagest counsel emanates from parents, it can be an entirely different matter. Still, I find it valuable to time-travel back and see how invaluable and sweet-sourced their advice was at the time. I often wonder if my daughters will ever have a similar chance to reflect on how well I know them.

This kind of advice from people I loved incited the voices sitting around my internal conference table. A big-voiced girl bellowed persuasively that I was invincible and the galaxy was the limit. The littlest girl, reticent among more commanding voices, softly reminded me of my brewing insecurities and deep fears. (She was, doubtless, the voice of my dad, however differently cloaked.) Not surprisingly, the girl with the big voice was most convincing, muffling the sounds of the others whose expressions of trepidation echoed faintly.

Over time, I began to learn that no inner voice, on its own, was the real me. Why? Because who would listen! I started to see that all of us are unique and complex combinations of our different inner voices, an assemblage that when in tune creates an exquisite harmony. Blind obeisance to any single inner voice throws us off. The other parts of us remain docile for only so long. Soon each insists upon a rightful place in the larger composition of our wholeness. Even when my inner-voice majority advocated moderation, it deferred inevitably to the loud cries of that one big voice. We need to be receptive to every inner voice finding expression. Someday, I hoped, I might unearth my core voice, or find consensus among them all. But right then I was swinging from another vine. The party had to go on.

I reached for the brass ring and met with Stuart Moldaw. Our connection, as when I met Bud, was instantaneous. Before we actually did, it seemed that we knew each other well. He was at once gracious, kind, shrewd, and wise. He had genuine interest in Gymboree. He liked the national franchise idea and wanted a business plan. He told me, "I like you, and I like the business. Go put together your growth model. If the plan makes sense, I am in." His encouragement dampened any remaining sense that I should act cautiously. He had visions for Gymboree that made my head spin. He envisioned products and stores and saw our brand as formidable as Playskool or Gerber, and even more synonymous with early childhood.

I worked tirelessly on a business plan with the same Chuck Bernstein who had invited me to speak at the Stanford Business School. Chuck was optimistic that, with my input, he could write a persuasive business plan. Trying to map the future this way was formidable. I knew we couldn't predict every event that might happen, and the past afforded us very little help in extrapolating how a national franchise rollout would work. The plan nonetheless called for explosive and purposeful growth, unlike the organic, ad hoc development that had brought us to our current place. Chuck, a masterful guide, was quite skillful in crafting a future that, he assured me, would one day become fact. I was having a hard time getting on board with this. To my novice eye, the projected numbers seemed random as a slot machine pull. He told me that I knew more than I thought, and that the numbers were not mere chance. The steep climb ahead had to begin with a trail map, an analogy he knew I understood (a nod to my experience as an avid hiker and off-road biker). I began to believe Chuck and the know-how that came with his experience. I did what I could to get myself comfortable, while I spat out specific states and sites where we would open and began to imagine the details becoming facts and not fable. The new VC-controlled world I was entering played this way. I was learning the ropes.

My fears subsided some as the plan began to take shape. The first jumble of numbers revealed we had a fighting chance. My job was to continue adding flesh to our skeletal business framework. I envisioned things like how many quality assurance representatives we would need per number of franchisees operating, and how a market development plan would unfold. I started to populate a U.S. map with centers in outlying New York suburbs like northern New Jersey, Westchester County, and Long Island. I added dots in Virginia near D.C., as well as in Miami, Detroit, and Chicago, and pretty soon we had accounted for all the major markets. I saw where marketing and public relations expenditures were nonnegotiable in order to get our brand out and find our target franchisees. I budgeted considerable dollars on that line item for many years to come. Chuck had the facility to make the numbers coincide with my storyline. I conferred with Bud about reasonable costs for new franchises to buy in, royalty fees, and other revenue numbers. I projected margin dollars for resale products at franchise sites. We spun our internal wheel of fortune, looking to land on a bottom line that would entice investment dollars.

The business plan, which took several months to complete, proceeded relatively smoothly. But as we approached the finish line, we confronted a few prospective questions about whether we could generate a return that would tickle the VCs, and I became disheartened. Worse, the caution counseled by my dad and George Gaber began to grip me. Maybe this was not a good idea after all. The familiar insecurity triggered my acting-out behaviors, which lay dormant when things went well.

It was not new for me to turn to food when I felt challenged and afraid. This binge-and-purge behavior had first emerged when I was in high school, and at the time it had seemed like a harmless vice. As life pressures mounted, though, these behaviors reared up more frequently. Over the years, I had misplaced the role of food in my life and sought solace in its company. What I ate, or did not eat, felt like something I could and should control. Eating for nourishment or even "normal" pleasure was becoming a privilege that was no longer mine to indulge. Not only did I begin to eat out of anxiety, I also felt panicky about my inability to stop. I felt ashamed of my insecurity and ashamed of my bulimic behavior.

I read about bulimia, and persuaded myself it might be a short-term solution to probable weight gain during this high-stress period. Sure enough, it "worked," and kept my weight "normal," allowing me, for the time being, to avoid facing the bigger issues of what was happening with me. I tricked myself into thinking that self-induced purging to solve overeating was a good fix for the "temporary" situation brought on by the pressure of the business plan, and that once the business got financed, the horror would cease. I told no one. I felt humiliated by my behavior, and blamed it all on insecurity. I convinced myself that the self-doubt bellowing inside me would fade as others continued to believe in me. And, as long as the outer world cooperated, the disease would recede into the background and deceive me into thinking I was "all better." The inverse notion of substituting the belief of others in me for self-love, however, served to strengthen the power of the bulimia as time went on.

It was becoming clearer that my ability to manage the regular stresses, strains, and upsets in my life was requiring me to turn to self-destructive behaviors, even though I continued to put forward a healthy exterior to everyone, including Bill. My struggles with food, weight, body image, and bulimia came and went. This vacillation confused me, insofar as things were under control when life was not "overpowering," a judgment that was entirely subjective. I was often perplexed and confused by the virulence and resilience of these problems. When things were on a roll, or I was able to handle a bump, the bulimia slumbered; when it felt like flood waters were cascading over me, it surfaced as a dominant force. All very confusing, to say the least.

Years later, I was inspired by something written by Viktor Frankl, a Holocaust survivor, in his book *Man's Search for Meaning*: "Our greatest freedom is the freedom to choose our attitude. Between stimulus and response, there is a space. In that space is our power to choose our response. In our response lies our growth and our freedom." For me, at this major professional and personal crossroads, the consistency of my freedom seemed distant, and I often felt adrift.

In May 1982, several months after I first met with Stuart Moldaw, USVP approved the business plan. As predicted, USVP had mounted a new $100 million consumer fund. The company allocated $300,000 to a national Gymboree franchise rollout, based on a $1 million company valuation. That gave me 70 percent and USVP 30 percent of the business. Bud joined the company officially. Donny Becker, the carpenter who had helped design and build the original Kindergym equipment, and his wife, Adrian Becker, a former JCC coworker of mine, became our first out-of-the-area franchisees, hoisting the Gymboree flag in the Los Angeles San Fernando Valley with a four-site territory, which flew high for 25 years! Ironically, Alice—the personification of Lady Luck who inspired the franchise rollout, in the end did not buy a franchise herself, for a variety of reasons. Her initiative, however, provided the fertile seed for Gymboree's subsequent great growth. George and Chuck joined our board, along with Sam Williams, our very own Stanford MBA CFO.

We were poised to turn the business plan into business fact. I was on a personal high, all potential distress (and my emerging pattern) submerged, thanks to selective attention. We were off and running—luck, heart, brains, belief, fresh funding, and all.

CHAPTER 7

∞∞∞∞∞∞∞∞∞∞∞∞∞∞∞∞∞∞∞∞∞∞∞

Do the Dream

THE NATIONAL FRANCHISE ROLLOUT proceeded with gusto. Bud Jacob filled his office with dotted demographic maps to highlight markets under development. Bud was more than a seasoned pro with great style and acumen; he was the likable dad type who figuratively held the hands of our young women franchisees as they got comfortable with their new undertaking. Working closely with me, he was the driving force behind this considerable operational phase.

We collaborated with each franchisee on market development plans that matched both their appetite and financial capacity for scale, and that also fit our long-term vision. The rollout's vigorous schedule required owners of multiple franchise sites to open new regional play center locations every six months. For example, a six-site territory took three years to ripen. The plan for a particular region could vary from one to eight individual franchised play center locations, from little mom-and-pop shops with a single location to significant small businesses in which an operator had as many as eight centers in her territory. We assigned each franchisee a quality assurance representative as the day-to-day point person.

My focus shifted to leadership and marketing. Like it or not, I was the role model the franchisees presumably wanted to emulate. The search for candidates who fit our model franchisee description required us to be creative outside our home market. We would grow new franchisees organically in a particular region once we had first seeded a new franchisee in that market ourselves. This allowed our replicating model to populate surrounding areas. I felt excited to figure out how to find initial franchisees in distant markets, still running on can-do candy. This was another special time in Gymboree's life; nothing felt insurmountable.

At Bud's suggestion, in 1984, I attended the International Franchise Association (IFA) convention in Chicago. I had much to learn about the industry and hoped to pick up cutting-edge techniques that would pack home easily, and I looked forward to networking and maybe even finding more mentors. Because our play centers represented a fresh and different kind of franchise business—certainly a far cry from the ubiquitous restaurant, hotel, and automotive franchises—and because we had appealing

Silicon Valley venture funding and national rollout plans, we were an intriguing new entry. That, presumably combined with our women-dominated culture and my enthusiastic participation in association meetings, prompted the IFA board to invite me to join them as a member. I accepted, a decision that proved invaluable. With my new sense of belonging, I was inspired to pursue an even grander dream: Gymboree as a national franchise phenomenon defined by interactive women-owned franchises, among which ideas would be exchanged freely. While we would not limit ourselves to women franchisees only, we sought to off-set, in our small way, the male-dominated aspect of the business world, where women were often excluded or made to feel less than deserving. At this time, women-led or women-dominated businesses were the exception. Those that existed were largely invisible on the national stage. This was not surprising, since our franchise rollout preceded the passage of the Women's Business Ownership Act of 1988, trailblazing legislation that broke down several barriers women faced in developing businesses, including the elimination of state laws that required men to cosign business loans to women.

Gymboree developed an invigorating franchise system that captured the business's key qualities: upbeat, affirming, collaborative, and operating under a "freedom flag" that challenged us to be unique. We encouraged each franchisee to try to create a balanced family and professional life that worked for her. For example, one woman might only want a single- or two-site territory where the operational demands basically translated into a part-time gig. Another might embrace growth opportunity and aspire to develop her territory into as many as eight sites, a full-time effort that would require hiring teaching staff and site managers, as well as developing a marketing presence in her operational communities. This policy led me to seek out and develop varied untapped markets of women—especially women who might have had little or no sense that they wanted to (or could) manage a Gymboree franchise, or any business for that matter. I was keen to figure this out, since on the other side of the solution my dream might become reality.

As chance had it, the Chicago public relations firm S&S Public Relations presented at the IFA conference and had the obligatory meet-and-greet booth. The S&S presentation was provocative and reminded me of the invaluable quality of free press, and how no amount of advertising could buy that kind of credibility. I was the proverbial choir for this particular song, since Gymboree had home-grown its company-owned sites and had located our franchisees in part based on benevolent free press or word of mouth. S&S senior vice president Betty Hoeffner impressed me instantly. I wanted Betty to work with me and Karen Anderson, our internal public relations person, to implement a winning press strategy in virgin markets.

I hired S&S and Betty, which was a deep-pocket outlay for us. The board empowered me to make those kinds of financial decisions with no oversight; I had their trust. In fact, as I was starting to understand, the VCs liked seeing a gutsy entrepreneur taking calculated chances where no research could project a quantifiable outcome. Betty built on the generous story our media coverage had already created: as the bellwether of a new industry, Gymboree was to pre-preschool what preschool had been to kindergarten in the 1960s and 1970s. This was weighty stuff, especially since it was the media, and not us at the company, that made this claim. Betty jumped all over this, amplifying the message in ways designed to better fashion our brand. Gymboree understood the great value of early age-appropriate learning experiences, such as those provided by the government-funded Head Start. We were committed to the critical foundations of the first three years of life, during which were laid the personal patterns for self-confidence, neural pathways for later learning, and good basic motor skills. Play is the way very young kids learn. Add to that the joy of parents experiencing this directly with their children, and what could be more wholesome and memorable?

We saw fitness as a family affair. Gymboree wanted parents to understand that interactive play built positive self-regard, and to experience that within the intimacy of the parent-child relationship. Joan Lunden, the long-time host of *Good Morning America*, captured this succinctly: "See how something that looks like just a lot of fun for kids can be a very beneficial learning experience for them and their parents as well." The *Wall Street Journal* lent its voice too: "Parents contend the program improves the child's balance, coordination and social skills. It gives babies and their parents a chance to mingle with their peers."

We offered unique products for socialization. Kids at Gymboree developed early habits of physical fitness that were comfortably coordinated for them and presented to them in ways that allowed the children to choose whatever activities or engagement suited them best. We understood that later academic learning was built on solid foundations of sequentially developed sensory systems. Our environment was ideal for kids to fulfill their natural drive for *doing.* Children learned to function individually and as an integral part of a group.

We continued to avoid making claims that kids would be better off for having the Gymboree experience—although we sometimes, depending on its depth, cited research that gave credence to our principles. Consider, for example, that all parents want their kids to grow up socially well adjusted. Research out of the Educational Testing Service from Princeton found that babies respond more favorably to the face of another baby than to that of an unknown adult. Babies and toddlers innately know that this other creature is similar, and they feel an automatic and kindred connection. Watching the smiles when quartets of six-month-old kids recognized their and other kids' faces in the Gymboree mirror, as they bounced on the large air-filled log, was priceless. This was early socialization at its most natural. We sensed its brilliance, its freshness—and its saleability.

We continued to refine our marketing message. In the mid-1980s, the times were changing as the personal computer era came into its own. Marketing mavens no longer believed that advertisers could deliver consumers in neat little packages crafted from simplistic formulas like age, education, and income—the once-gospel demographic trilogy. The Stanford Research Institute (SRI), our neighbor to the south, introduced into mainstream marketing a virtual new testament for Madison Avenue: psychographics, a field that originated in the 1950s and 1960s and studied the values, interests, lifestyles, and personalities of consumers, and examined how these and other factors influenced buying habits. Available for purchase, the data provided businesses and advertisers with insights into how to locate and market to subgroups, as well as sophisticated maps with census tracts that differentiated between demographics and lifestyle. Because people of a similar psychographic segment tend to congregate around like-minded people (to an extent greater than those with similar income or education), companies could customize sales pitches for the same product and more efficiently reach targeted consumers.

These new insights became critical to our pitch. It was no longer enough to know that our consumer was highly educated and had a relatively high disposable income. We discovered Gymboree attracted a more creative type, open to new ideas. Cutting-edge thinkers, as it were. Buying this information was wise. We massaged and integrated it into our press-release messages. The bait was alluring. We saw our story taken up almost everywhere we told it. I adored being part of this pioneering of marketing ideas that blended so well with our inherently fresh business program. We were benefiting from vibrant momentum.

The board stayed enthusiastic about franchise expansion, well aware that we might miss our financial numbers any given quarter. Stuart Moldaw and Linda Gordon Brownstein (of Montgomery Securities, our second major investor, who became our newest board member—at my request—in order to give the board some gender balance) were admiringly enthusiastic. They marveled at Gymboree's becoming a well-known and trustworthy brand. It had, I dare say, a gold-standard quality, despite how our relatively small revenues compared with our grand image. I was immensely proud, but I tried to keep my ego in check and focus on building Gymboree. We continued to target new markets and focused S&S on placing media stories in those markets. Watching this formula implemented thrilled me.

We established a foothold in the East Coast, first with the New York Metro market. That way, we reasoned, we would stay visible in the ever-important New York media marketplace, which I hoped would help prevent us from being ladened with an unflattering characterization like "an offbeat California phenomenon." The risk of being cast as something outside the mainstream was a real fear. It was smart, we thought, to ensure we stayed on the expansive and credible screen of the Big Apple.

From our new position on the Eastern seaboard, we laid claim to more markets across the country. We opened franchises in Philadelphia, Pittsburgh, Boston, Miami, Connecticut, D.C./ Virginia, Chicago, and the Detroit suburbs, and then extended to Kansas City, Houston, and Dallas. Soon, opportunities sprang up in Atlanta and various cities in Colorado, Arizona, and Nevada, to name just a few. Before long, we were operating or selling territories for future expansion in all the major markets and more. International expansion came organically, and before long we found ourselves in France, Australia, Canada, and Mexico. While generating this growth was not easy, it seemed to come with something of a natural, almost self-executing flow.

The media flattered us at every turn, fortunately, and continued to trumpet the mantra that we were becoming the new pre-preschool industry. We started to see more and more imitators and competitors: the ultimate flattery. This represented an actual cultural shift. Gymboree was becoming ubiquitous, and along the way changing the community-building landscape for young moms.

We were also entrenched in the national conversation about new consumer industries. The press seemed smitten not only with how we had created a unique early childhood must-do experience, but also with our new business model, which struck many as being as innovative and fresh as our original concept. Somehow we had birthed twins, worthy both of business pages and lifestyle section coverage. We began to get good copy in magazines like *Newsweek*, *Time*, *Fortune*, *Inc.*, *Entrepreneur*, and *Adweek*, as well as hybrid-type stories in outlets like *People* and *Us* magazines. We also appeared on the business pages of the *Wall Street Journal*, *USA Today*, and numerous local newspapers. In this way, the media helped expand the perception of Gymboree from preschool innovator to meaningful voice in glass-ceiling conversations. I was promoting these ideas on the talk-show circuit, expounding about women in business and how Gymboree was developing business opportunities for women and young moms in particular. I appeared on many of the major talk shows of the day: *Live with Regis and Kathie Lee!*, *Sally Jessy Raphael*,

The Today Show, and *CBS Morning News*—as well as several local shows in major markets.

I felt like a maverick riding the first wave of the women's movement in a world where I had, to this point, experienced virtually no pushback from men. On the contrary, the board, which was all men save Linda Brownstein and, for a short stint, Nancy Glaser of USVP, regularly championed me. They were a great source of affirmation, as were our bankers, lawyers, and the other men involved in the business. I felt on top of the world, albeit mindful of the cautionary advice of my media-savvy husband not to get too puffed up over the press and start believing the print.

In hindsight, this kind of media updraft is no longer possible today. Social media has not only changed our social interactions, but also robbed the traditional major media giants of the kind of clout we benefited from at Gymboree. Nor do customers rely on traditional media for credibility. It is as if we have shifted from trusting faceless journalists to giving more credence to real people like you and me. We're more likely to endorse any kind of social media over traditional media, which is increasingly viewed with a skeptical eye, save a few venerable outlets. Indeed, I am sure Gymboree could not be built the same way today.

While soliciting press was primary, it was not the only part of our marketing strategy. We hatched an advertising concept that should be an Ivy League MBA class case study for its uniqueness, or so I thought. Many promising available markets, we believed, were home to women who might not know they wanted to own a Gymboree franchise, or know that they possessed the potential to own any kind of business. We imagined that we could somehow find and attract these women. To do so, we initiated a campaign to reverse-market to them through their *Wall Street Journal*–reading husbands. These would become our only paid ads. Written as advertorials—a paid ad in editorial form—they highlighted the unique story of a particular Gymboree franchisee, in her own words, and spelled out the keys to the opportunity in the text: fulfillment, support, success, all could result just from owning a Gymboree franchise. We thus touted Gymboree's compelling and worthwhile business opportunity to the *WSJ's* male readership, promoting the national franchisor standing behind each franchisee; the household-name brand; the developing political currency of women-owned and -operated businesses; and the subliminal message that men, locked down in primary breadwinning positions, could become vicarious entrepreneurs through their capable wives. The play was that men would read the advertorial and think, *Now that is for* my *wife!*

When run from a home office, a Gymboree franchise allowed women to balance family focus with professional ambition. Franchisees could work at naptime, school time, or bedtime. They could teach themselves or they could hire teachers. We assisted each Zee with business development in order to help her realize her financial aims. The *Wall Street Journal* ad strategy revealed this untapped market, as men began calling to request the franchise information packet. Once they read the glowing press we included with the franchisee application, these men's wives would warm to the idea. And, as hoped, their interest really heated up once they spoke with operating Zees. We obtained a number of franchisees as a result of this strategy. Once a market was opened in an area, we stopped the regional ad in the *Wall Street Journal* and grew the market by tapping into the tried-and-true grassroots resource of existing Gymboree customers.

Our marketing strategy had a third main prong: the "See America Tour," my description for my travel schedule in those franchise rollout years. Prior to inviting potential franchisees to California to vet their candidacy, I visited many different markets to talk about who we were, why we existed, what we stood for, and what we were looking for in a franchisee. I scheduled tours almost monthly, meeting with potential franchisees in group settings across the nation. In each location, I typically met with anywhere from six to twelve women whom our franchise director, Linda Rasmussen, in consultation with Bud Jacob, had "prequalified." The various markets were rich with energetic and capable women. The face-to-face meetings brought a personal touch emblematic of our mission.

Once the meetings concluded, I informed the home office whether I thought a California visit made sense for specific franchisee candidates. We were loath for them to visit if I did not foresee a good fit. There was another expression of initiative required of the potential franchisees. After my presentation, the subsequent Q&A, and whatever follow-up due diligence they wanted to do, each needed to approach Gymboree in earnest again. We did not chase. We saw Gymboree as a business of passion. The good news was that those tours typically compelled a flurry of visits to California.

We considered the franchise-franchisor relationship a marriage: a long-term relationship that deserved rigorous approval standards. When candidates visited California (at their own cost) to discuss the franchise opportunity further, we would spend the better part of a day with them. They visited a center, met the franchise team, and toured the offices. The visit finale was a late lunch with the management team in my office. Breaking bread together around my hand-hewn pine conference table allowed us to see if we had that ever-important "family fit" to warrant looking at a market plan and drawing up contracts.

In the final stage of the process, six of us would meet to discuss the candidate's suitability for our franchise system. No Star Chamber, this was meant to be a heartfelt exchange of feelings, insights, questions, and projections about what life with the candidate might bring in terms of cohesiveness and success, as we defined it. We were intently focused on this dynamic, as culture was so important to us. Each of us six had veto power, meaning we had to be unanimous in selecting the candidate. All in or no go, no exceptions. We were resolutely committed, even in times of cash-flow difficulty, to welcome only those we were confident could succeed and also be a good fit for our culture. We knew inviolate adherence to this requirement risked our losing a solid candidate here and there, but we were committed to our exacting standards. This was emblematic of how we grew as a company, too. I believe our staff felt enormous loyalty to Gymboree not only because they had skin in the game via stock options, but also because they were involved in critical decisions. It was my nature to work best when everyone harmonized. I tend to think most (if not all) of us work best with a style that fits who we are, rather than who we think we ought to be.

In many respects, Gymboree was like a work family helping hundreds of children to flourish. It didn't matter that I was a contemporary of most Gymboree moms and franchisees. Plus, the media's image of me—far removed from the reality of my internal turbulence—cloaked me in protective privacy. My eating disorder, while ever present, seemed to recede during much of this period, as I felt so creative and inspired, and my energy was at an all-time high. The demon peeked out enough to remind me it had not receded altogether. For now, though, it was manageable.

The Gymboree world was full of joy. The families we served loved the classes, we had high repeat rates that continued to increase, and our franchises were generally profitable and happy. The Zees were proud of their contributions to their communities and were a source of pride for us all. Our success was the ultimate sum of the successes of each franchise operation and the happiness of all the kids and parents who attended. We were doing what we loved, making a difference in people's lives, and giving women opportunities to have their own businesses to boot.

We continued to extend our reach to new audiences. Child development was a hot topic, and if we could become a bigger part of the mainstream conversation, we could achieve even greater market penetration. We conceived a national syndicated column and persuaded the prestigious United Media Enterprises (UME), a large newspaper syndication service operating under United Feature Syndicate and the Newspaper Enterprise Association, to become our distribution vehicle. Their reputation preceded them, as they were touted as the best. They represented the famous *Peanuts* comic strip, as well as *Garfield* and other evergreen properties. UME exhibited excitement about our property, as it was called in the business, and they distributed our columns to what eventually amounted to 250 newspapers and to licensing agents. We were psyched, as you can imagine. Karen Anderson, with her master's degree in child development, had the credibility and writing talent to both pen our column and oversee our growing public relations efforts. The media saw us as experts in child development, ambassadors of learning through play. Gymboree was gradually becoming synonymous with what was good for kids. Or, as the *People* magazine article headline put it: "Move over Romper Room: All the Best Babies Come to Boogie at Joan Barnes' Gymboree."

Our columns covered everything from how babies develop language by making sounds to how exercise and physical play are essential in children's early years. We discussed the need for complicated nervous systems to develop sequentially, beginning with receiving and breaking down sensory information gathered from sound, light, and texture, and, of course, from all kinds of movement. Columns discussed topics like whether there was such a thing as too much play, whether you can push a child too much,

the importance of reading to your child, and so on. Each column advanced the Gymboree mission that play was "child's work"
and children learned while they had fun. The column reached
secondary markets and gave Gymboree wide name recognition
outside areas where we had franchise play centers. We increased
our visibility in these smaller markets with virtually no money
and little effort. Our national credibility grew exponentially.

By 1986, Gymboree had reached some significant milestones
since the initial venture capital funding in 1982. System revenues
exceeded $15,000,000. We were an international company with
more than 400 franchisees operating in more than 30 states
and 6 foreign countries. We had transitioned from a concept to
a local community service, and then from a community service
into a business, raising nearly $2 million in operating capital
from venture funds that believed in us. We were deeply rooted in
the business world.

This progress, and the financial success that came with it,
had me giddy. Building the franchise business marked the most
expansive part of Gymboree's growth. If it had been today, when
monetizing a business is often put off seemingly ad infinitum,
I might have felt more relaxed. In that regard, we were behind
our time. As it was, I felt charmed: I was in my mid-thirties with
two children, happily married, and spearheading the growth of
what appeared to be a robust, innovative business. The potential
seemed boundless. I was evolving, or so I was described, from an
entrepreneur to a "businesswoman." In truth, though, I was at
odds with that new handle. By my lights, once an entrepreneur,

always an entrepreneur. While I was far more seasoned and skilled than I had been in the JCC days, my passion for the Gymboree mission rendered me a different animal than the business professionals with their exportable expertise and operational skill sets. Within the parameters of my defined space, I felt invincible and empowered—but for Gymboree, and not for business per se.

I wondered, though, whether the dichotomy between entrepreneur and businesswoman would ever become more pronounced, and how I would be able to acclimate to that division. For the time being, though, I was still learning and filling both roles. Whether I could continue in those dual roles, or how I would fare doing so when the divisions became deeper, remained to be seen.

CHAPTER 8

∞∞∞∞∞∞∞∞∞∞∞∞∞∞∞∞∞∞∞

Your Own Press: To Believe or Not to Believe

THE GYMBOREE HOME OFFICE was south of the San Francisco airport and adjacent to international shipping giant DHL. The cream-colored cement-block building exuded dreariness, but inside, it palpitated with vibrancy. By 1986, we were an ebullient ensemble of 25, and the comings and goings of franchisees created a constant office buzz. Women at Gymboree mostly wore casual attire, often sweats, long before dress-down Friday was in vogue. The low-key dress code went a long way toward creating goodwill with the staff.

When we needed to stand up for our lofty mission, however, we suspended casual. The office doubled as our on-site franchisee training center, with each training event lasting a week or more. We also entertained franchisee candidates every week and held board meetings and other professional events. In these cases we honored decorum, well aware of the expected protocol of traditional business attire. We maintained our intimate family culture while respecting conventional etiquette.

We tried to ensure that the entire staff was engaging and courteous to everyone who stepped into our office; we strove to leave positive impressions, a feeling of belonging, as at the Gymboree play centers themselves. We hoped our home office conveyed a vibe that left visitors wanting to come back, or better yet, to never leave.

Despite our cherished informality, we kept heads-down focused, even on busy training weeks. Bud Jacob and his real estate team developed rollout plans, and Karen Anderson worked public relations magic as she and Betty from S&S filled my calendar with constant media interview opportunities. Julie Arvan, our one-woman product development squad, created new take-home products to be offered at the play centers. The quality assurance staff members, under the watchful eye of Linda Rasmussen, the Mother Superior of the franchise business, were in and out of the office, visiting franchisees in their locations to review their performance, introduce compliance standards, and aid them to achieve good results. Our hallmark was a quality system we embraced wherever we operated.

Most days, salt air wafted down from San Francisco Bay and shrouded the exterior of our offices. Some mornings, I felt the tug to linger near the bay before the workday drew me into its stimulating vortex, torn between my dual passions for nature and Gymboree. I sniffed the sea air and reveled in the damp chill on my skin from the coastal fog blanketing the ridgeline. Sometimes I could be lost for a few moments recollecting the chilly Midwestern mornings of my childhood. When something moves us, I don't think time softens its power. Despite those moments of welcome distraction, I was always excited about my Gymboree day. My relation to Gymboree had overtones of a love affair. The business captured my heart, and I surrendered to the intoxicating power of entrepreneurism.

My love extended to our growing Gymboree family. The people I worked with, the franchisees, and the families we served, floating around me in concentric circles of commitment and care, were changing the way the world interacted with infants and toddlers. We were affecting countless lives. Gymboree was an innovator in the marketplace and approaching a tipping point. I can't be sure when we transformed from being *the hip thing to do* to simply *what you do*, but once we turned that corner, it felt *really* good, even if not scientifically measurable.

Talk about being on a roll: out of the blue—the Hollywood hills, actually—we received an unsolicited product placement from the 1987 Diane Keaton movie *Baby Boom*. In the film, Keaton plays a hard-driving management consultant with no time for anything but her full-throttle career. Without warning, she becomes saddled with responsibility for a toddler after her cousin dies. Her new twin jobs—as mom and executive—inundate her as she struggles to learn how to raise a child in highly competitive

Manhattan while keeping apace of her rarified-air friends. One day, as she sits in an Upper West Side park, a trio of other moms pummels her with questions about what upwardly mobile steps she has taken to help her child. Has she signed up for this or that class? And then this: "What about Gymboree? Does she attend Gymboree?!" Her response betrays a feeling of being chastised for not knowing that Gymboree is the baseline for *all* moms. Indeed, what kind of mom would NOT go to Gymboree?

Baby Boom helped solidify our credibility. It was a cogent example of what Malcolm Gladwell illustrated in his book *The Tipping Point,* which showed how a series of incremental changes can become momentous enough to spawn a major, pervasive change. Gymboree was no longer subject to the fickle momentum that marks a fad. You can imagine how we reveled in this unanticipated affirmation. We had every reason to believe we had arrived at the magical tipping point. This was about as good as it gets: to become almost as well known as a Kleenex or Xerox—and without asking, paying, or even knowing we'd become so.

Despite all this media validation, we could not lose sight of our obligation to deliver a traditional bottom line. And, sure enough, as we basked in the glow, my magic carpet ride had a rough landing. I realized that our franchise business model, even while it was fueling worldwide expansion, had a fatal flaw in terms of delivering on investor expectations. We were trapped in a catch-22: parents, babies, and toddlers loved the classes and the franchisees were profitable, but in stark contrast, the parent company could not generate (and would not generate, regardless of the number of franchisees) a return on investment (ROI), never mind a consistent one. The formula—our growth notwithstanding—would never produce an economy of scale of real consequence. This was because the franchises' revenues, and thus their royalties to the corporation, were insufficient to cover the revised expenses necessary to support successful franchise operations. What we learned we had to spend to maintain and grow the community's profitability resulted in costs that far exceeded any reasonable Gymboree corporate budget.

Our main misstep had been that we had not anticipated the extent to which franchises would need quality assurance support for their ongoing success. Increasing royalty fees was no solution, for that would plow the Zees into the red—moreover, selling more franchises was contingent on current franchisees' profitability and satisfaction with the parent company's support. Compromise was not an option. We could survive as a break-even business, but the investors had not financed us to tread water for eternity. As a venture capital–infused company—unlike a business financed with personal funds or money from friends and family—expectations were all about ROI. I harked back to the sage (and prescient) words of George Gaber that once I took venture money, life would change in myriad ways. One of those changes had arrived.

The VCs, while not thrilled, hung tough, and directed that we focus hard on figuring out how the company could deliver an investment return. It was no overstatement to say we were on the verge of becoming a VC's worst nightmare. From their vantage point, better that we not chug along making payroll like a nice mom-and-pop business. Failure at least would allow them to shut us down, as they customarily do with almost half of the companies in which they invest. Venture firms hope that one company in their portfolio will spring the Big Win, a la Apple or Sun Microsystems, or more currently, Facebook or Twitter. Another few companies are expected to return a healthy four to nine times their investment. But virtually none tread water in perpetuity without any chance for investor exit. We were becoming that virtually none.

At the time, it all still seemed mostly in my grasp: my marriage, raising my family, and growing the business. I sometimes fancied myself Super Woman, capable of fixing any problem, no matter how formidable. I would figure it out. Trust me. At the same time, especially given the magnitude of the challenge, the fear of failure haunted me. It also fueled my motivation. I was resolute that no matter what the setback, what anyone said, what the numbers or markets showed, no matter what, Gymboree would not go down under my stewardship. Failure was not an option. It was not something I would consider.

Internal questions about my self-avowed invincibility, though, slowly slithered into my mind. Were they generated by my unwillingness, or inability, to give heed to all my different inner voices, to do what I call "listening in"? Or, did the internal voices all concur that failure was not an option? In truth, my internal naysayers gained little recognition because I refused to listen to their perspectives. At the time, I was unclear why no inner voice spoke of an exit strategy framed in any terms other than failure. That word, "failure," was plenty loaded for sure. After all, check out the statistics for all companies: some 50 percent of start-ups fail the first year, regardless of source of funding (e.g., VC, angel, family, friend, or self), and as many as 25 percent of those remaining join them over the next five years. This translates roughly to a 25 percent survival rate. So with a business failure, I would have been in good company, which of course is a place misery loves.

My natural zeal to project a competent, in-charge image complicated things. I operated out of the misguided notion that if you looked good on the outside and pleased others, you were rendered whole. I desperately wanted my interior world to match the exterior, and I kept clutching to the false hope that if I tried hard enough, it would. I didn't know if I could bear up under the cloud of failing the investors. Or was it personal failure that haunted me? I struggled then to find the kind of inspiration I would later discover and embrace in the astute words of Anna Quindlen: "If your success is not on your own terms, if it looks good to the world, but does not feel good in your heart, it is not success at all."

I poured my most vital energy into the save-the-company bucket. My kids seemed to be bearing up OK under the wings of their unorthodox mom who worked and traveled a lot. Even though our steady live-in au pairs oversaw much of the kids' school days, I was home on the weekends attending soccer games and doing all the essential family stuff, and our regular cabin getaways made for unifying family time. Only the distant future would tell me if my absence had impaired them any more than my presence might have. I had conflicts, of course. But I chose what I was doing.

Bill and I we were good partners and role models for sharing family responsibilities. While not Mr. Mom, Bill was as involved as I could reasonably desire. The three of us—Bill and I and our live-in nanny, who was like a big-sister figure in our home—reflected a type of new world order for working-parent families.

Having rationalized that my family was fine, I focused on solving the pending Gymboree crisis. We pondered a retail play, a product line that would capture our culture and further entrench our brand. Carolyn and BBDO mined the market research. Their work revealed compelling positive brand recognition: almost 70 percent of people in geographic markets where we had Gymboree play centers, and 50 percent of others among our target markets, knew our brand. The board reasoned that a corporate partner made sense, and they tasked me to run the idea by Don Fisher, the founder and CEO of the Gap, probably the most powerful retailer in the country, if not the world. My charge: persuade Fisher that Gymboree could be an asset to the Gap. Mindful that just getting an audience with Fisher was a flat-out tough assignment, I steeled myself.

I prepared heavily for my meeting with Fisher. I wanted to be able to field all difficult queries and dash any doubts with ready responses. The more I prepared, the more confident I became. When the day came, I went in with major jitters, yet I was able to regale Fisher about our culture, press, research, and unique customer loyalty, which I maintained would lead us to the retail promised land. I talked a mile a minute, and he seemed amused.

Fisher agreed that our existing brand awareness and loyal customers gave Gymboree a big boost. He said, however, that he was already planning to launch Gap Kids and thus was not interested in a Gymboree relationship. Great—not only did he lack interest in an alliance, but the Gap would also be a competitor if we entered the retail market. And of course they did start Gap Kids, and soon after introduced Baby Gap, too. Stuart Moldaw (who sat on the Gap board) told me I had impressed Don Fisher though, a man who, the lore went, did not impress easily. This encounter gave me confidence I could deliver in a big moment before a tough audience should the opportunity arise again. It also reinforced the value of comprehensive preparation.

I figured that at this point our board—comprised primarily of our venture capital backers—would not get behind any new strategy that required a "significant raise" of any new investment money. I was correct. Thus, we relegated retail to a remote back burner. We needed to take meaningful action that did not require an infusion of significant capital. This led us to licensing, which seemed a natural way to build on our existing business. It was a logical choice. Licensees shouldered the major capital investment burden and profited from our brand awareness and trust. This presumably could give us entrée to other product categories in the children's marketplace. Consumers, the argument went, would prefer to buy products with the Gymboree name rather than another, as our brand enjoyed widespread credibility.

A good analogy was Weight Watchers. Founded in 1963 by New York homemaker Jean Nidetch, Weight Watchers began as a service business to assist people with weight loss and maintenance. It evolved into a combination service and product business, licensed by Heinz, with brand recognition that appealed to a segment of the market well beyond those core Weight Watchers customers who participated in the company's supportive membership meetings. I was convinced that licensing—dependent on the same kind of brand recognition that Weight Watchers enjoyed—could generate the same success for Gymboree. The board reacted favorably.

Before we patted ourselves on the back, we had to secure excellent licensees in categories that gave us sufficient oversight over product quality and marketing efforts and full approval of product merchandising. UME signed us up to extend services from our media-licensed column to larger product categories. This buoyed our confidence. We piled up some stellar licensees, such as Random House, A&M Records, Dakin (for plush products), Karl-Lorimar Scholastic (for video), Healthtex (for clothing), and Connor (for large home play equipment and toys). Gymboree, we believed, would produce a very promising return on investment as a result of this strategy. After contracts were signed, product development and marketing moved forward swiftly.

As we advanced in this new direction, I found still more gratification from this exterior success. I dug myself deeper into the misguided notion that this success would fulfill me. The venture capitalists fed this delusion, as they insisted I would be the rare entrepreneur to take a business from conception to public-company status. The national press coverage, combined with the incessant message that I had the perfect life, also fed my sense of invincibility.

In licensing, as I learned, the "sell-through," the products that sell in the marketplace, is vital to the success of the licensing deal. If consumers do not buy big out of the gate, the whole operation is likely to fizzle, particularly if the licensees are not patient and lack commitment for the long haul.

As it turned out, Gymboree was not hot in the licensing market; in fact, we were downright lackluster and delivered uninspired performance. Some at the company believed our licensees mishandled how our brand was presented to retailers, notwithstanding all our good press. Others claimed we needed a TV show and viewer following to make licensing a success. Who knew where the truth lay or whether there was blame to cast? We could debate the point ad nauseam, but the bottom line was that the retailers did not reorder and the licensees declined to renew their licensing contracts. Less than a year after we embarked on this new road to success, the licensing program croaked, except to sell off dust-gathering inventory. The exception was our large play-equipment line, which performed well enough at Toys "R" Us that our licensee, Connor, continued with its license. That success was not enough to call licensing our new strategic path to greater profits.

The fear of failure gripped me stronger than ever. Were we en route to becoming a major euphemistic "write down"? As best I could fathom, we needed a downright miracle.

CHAPTER 9

∞∞∞∞∞∞∞∞∞∞∞∞∞∞∞∞∞∞∞∞∞

You Said What?

THE DEMISE OF THE LICENSING GAMBIT signaled that I had to find another solution before the life got sucked out of our current momentum. It was time to find a real corporate suitor, an established business that could extract value from our brand and integrate us into its family. A strategic buyer. Someone was out there, I was convinced, who believed fundamentally in our brand and possessed the financial firepower and visionary mindset to develop us. Many respected companies operated in the children's marketplace where the Gymboree brand could add value. I availed myself of the wise words of Stuart Moldaw: "A lot of business success is being on the right corner at the right time, when the bus you need goes by and you decide to jump on it."

Were the vibrations I felt the rumblings of our bus chugging down the road toward us or did they portend something worse?

My sense that Gymboree's mission remained unfulfilled piggybacked on my strong fear of failure. My resolve hardened each time we stumbled. Even though our circumstances hinted that the time to hoist the white flag might be near, no one spoke about it. We were like those families who keep the prognosis from a terminally ill family member, mostly because it is so hard to live without hope. I believed that it was more than just hard to live without hope—it was unproductive, even self-fulfilling, to act in negative ways, because we often create the reality we believe. Better put, it is almost impossible to obtain a positive outcome if you are coming from a negative place.

Realism, though: that just makes sense. At this juncture, I knew that Gymboree might be on borrowed time. Still, I did not cower. On the contrary, I held on to the possibility that the key to our long-term success could be found. What is more, my proven willingness to sacrifice sleep, sanity, and savings might aptly define—with tongue only slightly in cheek—the core requirements of an entrepreneur. I had a job to do, and I felt that completing the job was essential. I would not surrender the ship.

I reviewed the facts in our favor in order to gain ballast while we bounced about looking for smooth waters. The franchise system, of itself, was strong. Gymboree's brand had earned trust in the marketplace. I had the confidence of our investors that I could figure this out. Montgomery Securities and USVP anted up for another round of financing, unfazed that Gymboree's brand cachet had not yet been monetized enough for an acceptable investment exit strategy. They continued to believe we could ascend to dominance. The thinking was that we needed only find the right partners. Having the support of the key board members was of immeasurable value to me.

Despite the optimism I expressed, I couldn't wipe out the feelings of rejection I sometimes confronted. I admitted, if only to myself, that I was afraid. My childhood lessons in hiding my insecurities and pasting on a charismatic face for the rest of the world served me well. The board wanted no other CEO, and the press demanded ever more interviews and stories, as we continued to build name recognition and brand awareness. But I asked myself if I was the right person to spearhead this next phase. And would there even be a next phase? I had doubts on both counts. Even though part of me longed to spill my insecurities, I hid them, as I was trained to do. "You will have no friends if you are not fun to be around," Mom had once told me. It was messages like that one, and so many others, that kept me from breaking silence now. I wanted so much to disclose my feelings of inadequacy. I was never so tough that tears were inaccessible, especially on my early morning walks before bracing for the day. I loved my work; I was just tired of feeling like I was in over my head. My world was split. To the outside, I stood staunch and full of belief and confidence. With myself—and, sometimes, with Bill—I gave in to my demons.

My eating disorder became stronger. I ate for comfort; I ate to punish myself for feeling I was out of my element; and I ate out of anxiety and frustration to control what I could. I did not eat behind closed doors, for that was not my style. I wasn't a binger, rather more of a steady type of eater, which helped mask my problem. My eating issues were easily hidden, especially because I looked so normal. I purged on a regular schedule, in secrecy, and I exercised obsessively, which kept me at a normal weight. I thought of any extreme behavior with food as just "one of those days." Many days, whenever franchise training was not in session, I taught an aerobics class for the staff. The press found this charming, like a grown-up version of Gymboree. No one suspected that it could be a telltale sign of my advancing eating disorder. I was developing a mild exercise addiction, but I presented myself to the world as a woman with excellent discipline and commitment to her well-being. I was complicit in this cover-up, and as a result my shame deepened.

I kept a huge metal bowl of popcorn on my desk, which beckoned hypnotically. I consumed little inconspicuous nibbles throughout the afternoon. The rhythmic reach and grab soothed me. Sometimes I savored my feeling of control when I picked up a single kernel. Other times, I was frightened by how out of control I felt when I couldn't stop eating those seemingly harmless morsels. The very faces of paradox, the popcorn kernels became both my allies and my enemies. I ate them for comfort. When I felt I had overdone it, spilling my guts in a toilet bowl somehow felt less exposing than opening my heart to another person.

Therein lay the cunning progression of my bulimia. Mine began when I was kid, with a few stolen cookies. My favorites as a child were chocolate chips made by our live-in, Lucinda, which she piled high in a Raggedy Ann jar. I learned to replace the bright red-mopped ceramic top gingerly so as not to be busted. No sooner had I perfected this ruse than my appetites changed. My predilection switched to spreading Planters peanut butter and Welch's grape jelly fastidiously onto a Jays potato chip. I saw the kinship between my potato chip routine and my popcorn pattern some 30 years later. These small, familiar acts seemed a benign, almost charming, compulsion as I got lost in the repetitive pattern while pondering the future of my business.

Gymboree was the first time I felt a personal sense of total core engagement outside of my love for my daughters and Bill. I couldn't imagine giving up the reins to the business anymore than I could give up my kids or my marriage. Abandoning the company would be like leaving a love affair in full bloom, shortcomings and all. I had to forge ahead, somehow.

Before the licensing strategy dissolved, I had met the head of product development at Hasbro at the big toy-industry fair in New York in the winter of 1985. At the fair, we had showcased our line of large home play equipment, our one clear winner. Buyers and company representatives buzzed about—Gymboree looked hot, especially because folks from Toys "R" Us crowded our booth and ardent media people were literally crawling on the equipment. We exuded "big property" promise amid the snapping photographers.

Like Stu said, timing is everything. Recalling the Hasbro product guy and the way he repeatedly circled back to our booth,

I contacted him and presented him with the same facts I had delivered when I met with Don Fisher of the Gap (ah, the virtues of the practice run). He wanted to put together a meeting in New York with the two of us and Stephen Hassenfeld, the CEO of Hasbro. Hassenfeld had done wonders with Hasbro since taking over the business after his father's death. Based on the research I'd done on him, I sensed he had an appetite for new frontiers. Our board authorized an exploratory meeting and, in a relatively brief time, I was face to face with Hassenfeld. More than attentive and polite, he was engaging, albeit playing it close to the vest about a possible alliance. I was confident, though, that Hassenfeld had liked what he heard. I reported all this to the board and urged that we pursue Hasbro as a suitor, and the board gave me the green light. Maybe Hasbro would have more patience with licensing, or be moved to develop the Gymboree brand as a separate toy division. We would see.

Hassenfeld flew me to Hasbro's Rhode Island headquarters in a private jet. Their team was psyched. We talked about Gymboree becoming a wholly owned Hasbro subsidiary. Quickly, due diligence began. While some at Hasbro harbored reluctance because the service aspect of Gymboree would represent a new market for them, most saw the long-term vision. After these discussions, which spanned a few months, the Hasbro board offered to purchase an initial 25 percent stake in Gymboree, with an eye toward acquiring a majority interest after that and moving toward an ultimate goal of total acquisition.

This suited me and it suited our board. The lawyers prepared the papers and we were set to sign on the dotted line. I headed to New York the evening before the scheduled closing. Joining me later would be Gymboree board member Linda Gordon Brownstein and our attorney, Jeff Saper of Wilson Sonsini Goodrich & Rosati, whose desk had always impressed me with its assortment of Lucite monuments to the public-offering deals he'd done. We anticipated a brunch the next morning to celebrate the signing before we headed back to San Francisco. While somewhat apprehensive that I would soon be reporting to a Hasbro corporate vice president, mostly I was ecstatic that Gymboree was about to turn the corner. Maybe it would turn out that with Hasbro I would be exposed as someone who was just winging it, and get replaced. That was fine. I took comfort knowing that the board and investors would have a corporate partner, and Gymboree would remain on course to making its big mark in the world.

Trying not to obsess about the future, I chilled in my New York hotel room reviewing franchise marketing plans for the first national ads that BBDO had created for publication in *Parents* magazine. I scanned the marketing plans while resting comfortably on the hotel bed. The plans surveyed market penetration and views per page. This part was pretty new to me and I was excited to learn about it. It would also allow me to work more with my friend Carolyn André from BBDO and showcase her considerable talents, plus spend some time together, which our respective busy careers had denied us of late.

The Zees loved Carolyn; she knew her stuff. We had recently formed a council to oversee spending money pooled between the Zees and "the Zor" (as franchisor, we were of course the Zor), a form of cooperative. The Zees-Zor council was emblematic of my vision for collaboration. The money in these coffers was enough to do something significant. Everyone had weighed in with views about this, as you might imagine. The cleverly created ads were research driven. The work of Carolyn and her staff included sophisticated black-and-white photography of kids with thought bubbles above their heads, thinking: "Mommy and I are finally relating on the same level," or "Definitely more fun than toilet training." They were clever and, I thought, superior to predictable color ads showing a Gymboree play center. Most understood that the ads were another expression of Gymboree's identity as innovator, and a good way to catch the attention of our highly educated, psychographically specific market.

As I was lost in thought about the upcoming Zee-Zor council meeting and the splendor of the national ad program to follow, my hotel phone rang unexpectedly.

> *Hello?*
>
> *Is this Joan Barnes?*
>
> *Yes.*
>
> *This is Carole Anderson. I am the senior vice president of corporate affairs for Hasbro.*
>
> *Hi Carole. I don't believe we have met, have we?*
>
> *No.*
>
> *Nice to meet you, Carole.*

I want to tell you, Joan, that Hasbro has changed its mind and we will not be executing the contract with you tomorrow.

Carole, I don't think I understand. You are what?

We won't be coming to meet you in the morning. We have changed our minds. We will not be doing the deal.

I'm sure there must be some confusion. I have people on a plane right now. Are they aware of this?

No. I am sure you will be able to tell them in time.

No one will be there tomorrow to speak with us?

That is right.

I am confused. We have the contracts; our lawyer and yours have approved all the changes.

Management no longer wants to do this deal. That's that.

OK. I think I understand.

Click. She was gone. I never heard from anyone at Hasbro again.

My heart beat at breakneck speed. My arms shook as if someone had tossed me into icy water. I began sweating. I was having trouble swallowing. I could not stand; when I tried, the room went black. Was I blacking out? I lay down and then remembered a trick from my childhood. I pretended; I went into my "refuse to believe" mode. I submerged reality and engaged the stabilizing force of denial. The Anderson call was a misunderstanding and "never happened." A passing moment of fear extended to a full-force waking nightmare. I gathered myself and got somewhat real. Tethered to what I could do, I called the Gymboree offices back in Burlingame and kibitzed about business as usual. When I hung up, reality overran me. My breath quickened, and I was flooded by monster shame, feeling it was all somehow my fault. I started to exhale in small increments the way I had in Lamaze breathing class, as if I were preparing to deal with birth contractions. Damn, if only a beautiful baby would arrive, instead of what felt like this mad rush into a dark abyss.

I didn't know what to do. I was way too ashamed and embarrassed to call anyone and tell them what had happened. Bill's instinct would be to "make it better," and without him present to hold me and comfort me physically, hearing his voice would act to make things worse. I flirted again with the insane thought that if I just said nothing, perhaps no one would know and it all might go away, as if it hadn't happened. I finally left a message for Linda to come to my hotel room after she arrived from JFK. When I saw her, I began to sob uncontrollably. She held and comforted me and told me it was not over. She still believed in the company and in me. I melted into her every word, even if my pained insides did not trust the sound of them. She had my back. That was a rare thing, and I treasured it—I needed her faith, her friendship. My connection with Linda holds strong to this day. Moments like these teach you what it means to have people standing for, by, and with you in tough times.

After a postmortem later that evening when Jeff arrived, we decided I would discuss the situation with Stuart and the staff in person when I returned to California. I needed a few days to sort out how to strategize where to go from here.

I covet a memento from that hellish day: the love and re-spect offered to me by Linda and Jeff, the humanity we shared with each other. While I remained uncertain and fearful for sure, I maintained a reservoir of hope to help me keep trying. Until then, nothing had really dispirited me. I was just taking my knocks. And like an indomitable boxer, I kept getting up. But this time, the mandatory eight-count had an interminable ring. What would the world look and feel like when I arose from the mat this time? I felt an overriding and palpable dread that both the company and I were headed lockstep on unalterable collision courses: me crashing with failure and self-doubt, and the com-pany propelled into the VC dump heap of investment write-offs. The balance of power among my inner voices was shifting.

CHAPTER 10

•••••••••••••••••••••••••••••••••••

What Impedes, Inspires

THE HASBRO DEBACLE left me traumatized and numb. As the jet from New York unloaded me on the West Coast, I wondered whether I would find enough strength and resilience back at my Gymboree base camp to tease some sort of silver-lining rally cry from this major setback. This was not just another tricky day at work; this was a crossroads. My leadership and my personal sense of balance were both on the line. I knew I had to find some way to produce a positive outcome after the sharpest challenge I had experienced as an entrepreneur. While at the moment I lacked the clarity to see how this could be accomplished, I knew a simple truth: what you water grows.

As I waited for my luggage at SFO, I reminded myself that for me, after any tough turn, comfort begins with asking the right questions—even if the answers don't leap out. This technique created space for me to gain patience and become grounded, and fostered a mind-set that served me well in unnerving times. For entrepreneurs, uncertainty is a way of life. As I ruminated, the buzzer sounded, alerting me to the impending cascade of luggage and resetting my focus.

En route to the Gymboree office in a cab, I decided I needed a full dose of springtime in the Sierra, where I hoped the mountain sunlight could endow me with fresh energy. What if, rather than diving deep into the problem-solving pool at the company, I instead reconnected with the American River bellowing down the canyon of Desolation Wilderness? Sometimes restoration calls for a complete power-down. Our family cabin, affectionately and aptly branded "the Cabin," sits snuggled among evergreens atop mammoth granite slabs that look down on that mighty river. Maybe you know that place where you feel a part of all things? The Cabin called to me, even though the timing seemed counterintuitive. I thought it could help me let go of my obsessive thoughts and nurture the patience I needed.

Before I could take leave, however, I had leadership responsibilities. I needed to tell the staff what had happened in New York, and I could not downplay the insult of Hasbro pulling the rug out from under us. I had an unexpected aha moment: what if I asked my staff to find a creative way out of the current impasse—without me? I had a loyal, creative, and competent team that consistently rose to the occasion. I was spent. I knew that if I jumped in with them for the next round of problem solving, I could be a fly in the ointment. What if I asked them to meet without me over the next few days and freed them to be unfettered in their brainstorming? We had a clear and shared sense of purpose; they had all the talent, drive, and commitment that were needed. I realized they represented our best bet to find our future direction.

As the cab approached the Gymboree office, my heart was in my throat about the impending talk, yet once I saw my team, my optimism returned.

"Welcome home!" they sang out in concert as I entered my office and found them gathered around my pine conference table.

Everyone was standing. I asked them to sit.

"So damn good to see you guys." I hesitated. "It wasn't what we expected; you got that much."

There was soft laughter around the table as everyone exchanged glances and we reestablished our familiar ease.

"OK, give us the dirt!" one requested.

"We are dying for the details," said another.

Bud cracked the ice as only he could: "We know it was a bust, but shit, how could they?"

"OK, you asked for it." I recounted the play-by-play, sparing few details. We were united in being crestfallen. The prospect of finding a corporate partner was off the table now. Everyone got that. Then I told them about my epiphany in the cab. I asked them to stage a creative session without me.

"I believe our future lies in the hearts and minds of this group, not in me. In fact, I am so drained I feel certain that great stuff will surface more easily without me around. Can I count on you to put these sessions together and see what comes out of them?"

The responses were unanimously affirmative. Hands clasped spontaneously. We exchanged nods and smiles. There was an obvious excitement; everyone in the room was stimulated by the prospect. They would give it their all. I was both eager for the outcome and grateful I could use my time at the Cabin for necessary rejuvenation.

Was this brilliant leadership? Sheer desperation? Entrepreneurial gall? An inappropriate delegation of executive duty? Or something else? While I had no B-school techniques to lean on, I had learned this much on the job: when colleagues in crisis feel empowered and trusted in a committed environment shaped by core team values, leadership that knows its limitations can stir a team to carry forth. Strong teams can thrive through hardship when people are assembled using sound hiring principles and share years of highs and lows together. Character and fit were always my first hiring criteria, and experience second. I knew this, too: what impedes can also inspire.

In fast-paced organizations where flexibility trumps all, there is no time to get bogged down by grandiose or competitive personalities. My idea for the best way to build a dynamic start-up was (and remains) to bring on the best possible people, define their roles smartly, and get out of their way, for the most part. Everyone—including the visionary, the entrepreneur, or the CEO—is eventually replaceable. After all, we were building a brand, not personal legacies. That company mission preempted all, and its well-being depended on loyal service and care.

My confidence in the staff fortified me for the Sierra respite. Bill, the kids, and I packed the Toyota 4Runner, headed northeast through Sacramento, and climbed toward Tahoe. The Cabin lies 20 miles west of South Lake in El Dorado County amid the gorgeous Desolation Wilderness. Fortunately, at ages ten and twelve, the girls still favored a Cabin trip over most anything. This tradition saw our days filled with hikes and swims in cold snow-melt lakes and our nights with parody productions of what had gone on during the day, often hilariously poking fun at Bill and me for doing things we never knew they noticed. Without a TV, the whole world unfolded for us. It is a priceless paradise that holds a special place in the girls' hearts to this day, as it does for the next generation, my grandchildren, who have experienced the same pleasures of sleeping under the stars, taking chilly swims, and singing around the campfire with guitars and s'mores.

The family reconnection energized me. We made our traditional stop en route at a joint called Sam's Place, where the girls played skeeball and other games on the peanut-shelled floor. I was surprised how good it felt to participate in this loud ritual, a counterpoint to the quiet of the natural surroundings. After awhile, Bill bribed them to depart this chaos with their favorite saltwater taffies. Hugging them both before we jumped back into the SUV, I was overcome with gratitude for my family. Everyone was happy, and we ascended the last leg winding up the scenic

Highway 50 to the Cabin. Upon arrival, everybody pitched in unpacking and setting up the outdoor sleeping pads and bags for later. We swam at our secret lake and mounted a few inflatable boats for the girls to paddle about in the pristine, glacier-fed waters. Bill and I stretched out on the granite slabs and barely spoke.

As night neared, we gathered on the deck for dinner, staring up at Frog Mountain, our nickname for a granite rock that resembles a frog on the faraway horizon. After, the girls chose a jigsaw puzzle. I swayed in the rope hammock on the deck, lulled by the constant river sounds. The Cabin remains so primitive because the U.S. Forest Service has mandated that it be unchanged since the 1930s. Imbibing the healthy mountain air imbued me with a sense of timelessness.

The process of recharging my belief in myself had begun. After a few days passed, the Hasbro nightmare slowly dissolved to a haze. While the future remained unsure, the events in New York no longer seemed like doomsday. But, as I was enjoying this chance to decompress, Nancy Bott, Gymboree's controller and back office jack-of-all-trades, showed up at the Cabin. Her family owns a similar place not far from ours where our two families often convene. This time, however, she had not come for a social visit.

While the staff continued to work on the project I had commissioned, Gymboree had immediate, short-term problems. The company was down to its last $50,000, enough to stay afloat for a month or two, at most. I had been treating our cash-flow problem like a passing hiccup because Hasbro had committed to infusing its new corporate partner with enough money to address this predicament after the deal closed. I was learning the hard way that financial planning based on an unsigned deal was not sound management. Nancy and I worked hard to conceive a stopgap plan to stay afloat. We hatched a no-nonsense plan that slashed head count and lowered the salaries of those who made it into the lifeboat. There was no other way.

Upon my return, I braced myself to reduce the head count, make pay cuts, and put some teeth into the contingency plan hatched in the Sierra. I no sooner got to my office than I made a startling discovery. Julie Arvan, our resident creative giant who ran product merchandising for the franchises, had placed on my desk a hand-drawn poster board. It was a complete mock-up of our proposed future: a bona fide retail operation. The poster depicted a featured Gymboree retail store in a top regional mall showcasing our line of kids' apparel, play equipment, and toys. Next to the store, Julie had sketched a Gymboree play center. The mock-up was powerful. Somehow, while the idea of Gymboree retail was not new—recall my earlier pitch to the Gap—the potential expressed in Julie's mock-up now shone with brilliance. Timing was everything, and the time had come.

At first I was frozen in place as I took it all in. Then, recognizing the significance, I grabbed the poster board and howled "Yes!" Drawn to the sounds of rejoicing coming from my office, others joined me, and we busted out in a crazy mix of tears and laughter. The staff felt validated and proud, deservedly so. My mind reeled; our dour future now showed glimmers of brightness like Sierra sunlight coming through the trees. Everyone knew this was still a long shot. Heads still had to roll, and those remaining would still see pay cuts. Nonetheless, the mood shifted from "what now?" to "this is it!"

I asked Nancy to prepare preliminary numbers with Julie's help. A few days later, Nancy and I visited Stuart Moldaw, now chairman of the board of directors and, as always, my dogged mentor. Stuart would provide a major threshold test of our new initiative; his hawk-eye for numbers and unaffected shrewdness could stop me dead in my tracks. When I met with him to float the retail proposal, I first gave him all the details of the Hasbro collapse. He was angry about their unprofessional treatment and dismissed the whole thing as a distraction: "Corporate partners are usually a pain in the ass anyway."

He was ready for the next part of the agenda, and I was much relieved. It was not the difficult conversation I had dreaded. I described how we were managing our cash-flow as a result of the lost Hasbro deal. He was impressed with the swiftness with which we'd axed overhead and our willingness to take a hit to our own salaries. We then moved on to our new retail strategy. He was all over the idea, which reaffirmed his own early vision for retail. He told us to build a rollout plan and call a board meeting with deliberate speed. If the plan made sense, he was in.

Stuart ended with a comment about Don Fischer and The Gap: "You know that The Gap is one smart company. They would not be heading into the children's market without firm research confirming it as a big play. Don may have made a mistake, Joan: we are Gymboree; we have the name in that market."

We left feeling like Tinker Bells, fairy dust and all. Our salvation was far from a done deal, but who knew that hitting rock bottom could lead to such a rejuvenating strategy?

One thing I knew about myself by now—when inspired, I felt no hesitation. Knowing we had to sell this to the board and the investors, and anticipating skepticism, I refused to give it anything other than my all. I had come to a career-defining leadership moment. We needed a well-defined path to a clear destination. Preparation was essential to generating confidence for all. I had to be prepared, I had to prepare my staff, and I had to prepare the board.

As we geared up, I defined roles carefully, tasking everyone according to her or his particular expertise to craft the applicable piece of the retail plan. We were seasoned pros. I was confident we could generate a superior and compelling business model. I was concerned about something else, however. Even in the routine workday, the pressure to perform can generate disputes or ruffled feathers. How much more could the staff endure laboring under severe time pressure with so much at stake, in an atmosphere where we had already suffered pay cuts and downsizing, and with no assurance we would survive this chapter? It had to be a challenge for many to justify continued commitment to a company demanding more hours for less pay, all while facing an uncertain future. Knowing this, I was extra attentive to the importance of affirming the effort of everyone throughout this process. I reminded everyone that tensions, conflicts, frayed feelings, and bruised egos are often the norm in this kind of pressure cooker, and to come to me immediately with any problem. We would sort out any difficulty. We all shared the same desire for success born of harmony. We would focus on getting back on track, guided by an overriding sense that we could and would succeed in a manner where all felt good about their contributions. Addressing the issues that arose provided a contagious and abiding sense of solidarity. One time-tested formula for success: assemble people who inspire each other, and who share values and a belief in a common purpose, and share the credit as a group.

After prodigious preparation, we were ready to face the board. While we brimmed with excitement, we curtailed any inclination toward overconfidence. I subscribe to the under-promise and over-deliver school. Despite how well the preparation process had gone, and how strongly we each felt about our particular contribution, we had to see all angles and be steeled for all tests.

I reviewed my presentation more times than I could count and knew the contents cold. The details, however, were not my concern. Stuart told me that while the specifics were important, it was better that they "sing." I got what he meant; we had arrived beyond the point where delivering a well-crunched financial plan could do the trick. The board would not embrace any presentation that promoted mere subsistence. This meant I had to do more than inform and persuade; I had to inspire.

While anxiety seemed part and parcel of the circumstance, I could ill afford to evince any sense we were in desperate straits. Past failures were irrelevant now—if anything, they were springboards for future success. The Gymboree mission was to improve the lives of countless children and adults and provide business opportunities for women. More than just knowing this, I *believed* it, and that belief is what I knew I had to convey with unconditional conviction. While it might not carry the day, its absence would doom us. I had to stir the board with my enthusiastic optimism about the future.

As I entered the meeting, the boardroom had a distinctly different feel. The normal back-and-forth banter was missing. There was awkwardness, an apprehension that bordered on impatience. I had hoped for help out of the gate, some rah-rah encouragement to get us started. Instead, the board members were subdued. I got a smile and greeting from everyone, but the smiles were tight-lipped and the greetings restrained.

I started with the conclusions, telling them in summary what I was about to tell them in detail. I was braced to confront residual questions about Hasbro before any new strategy could take center stage. However, no one said anything about Hasbro and I chose not to address the subject. So, with little ado, I launched into the strategy pitch, marshaling its well-documented research and stylish graphic representation. I paced a little in finding my rhythm, making sure I made eye contact with someone at all times. As momentum built, I gained confidence and began to speak from the heart as well as from the charts and tables. Before long, I sensed I had their rapt attention, as intermittent nods of the head appeared across the room.

We peppered the board with apparel drawings, statistics on name recognition, and a proposed site location. The business plan included a two-year rollout plan with specifics as to the funds needed for the next twelve months. We had mock-ups of some apparel and drawings for the rest; compelling architectural renderings of the storefront and merchandising fixtures; and a financial model with expected annual income and expenses. I presented for more than an hour. All our investors remained present. I was on my game, I knew; the board was engaged and my story was compelling. While, again, retail was not a new idea, this time we were selling timing as much as anything else. This was Gymboree's moment. All the earlier fits and starts had worked in our favor, preparing us for this day, our moment to act. Gymboree had established its niche over the past ten years, building trust and respect via our network of franchised, inter-active play-and-music centers aimed at the infant, toddler, and preschool markets. We had earned it.

As expected, the board pummeled us with incisive questions. They hit us with the usual spate of "what ifs," which I handled with illustrations of market trends, the specifics of our powerful market research, and the sensible nature of the incrementally paced program we advocated. I spun each "what if" as more hy-pothetical than real, with risks minimal throughout. *Not to worry, folks, we are good.* I dared not say we had no choice and were up against a wall, which—while obvious to them—would betray a lack of confidence. A desperate entreaty would not inspire this group. Again, while I knew the details were important, today they weren't as important as my tone of voice, the spark in my eye, and the passion in my heart.

The board lobbed its most daunting and direct challenge my way. What made us think retail would work when licensing had failed? This one I had anticipated. I explained that the Gymboree story must be told our way, in our own physical environment, which licensing, by definition, could not do. I reminded the board how prescient Stuart Moldaw had been, four years earlier, in projecting retail as our ultimate future. I amplified my earlier point that we could gain substantial comfort from the powerful research we had performed on our brand, which is what had compelled so many prestigious licensees to sign on in the first place. We had the most enviable and coveted market one could imagine. The educational statistics on our client base told us that 28 percent had graduate degrees and almost another 40 percent were college graduates. And, of the remaining 32 percent, another 27 percent had some college background. This was powerful and uncommon market data. Our client base was largely composed of trendsetters who expressed their convictions with the pocketbook, spending more per capita on their children than any other demographic. Even Gap Kids, with all its advertising muscle, would have to find ways to cultivate the market we already owned. Heads nodded again and board members glanced at each other, affirming the power of these statistics.

Then things hit a tough point. Arthur Fremlin, formerly the president of a major retailer, who had recently joined USVP, asked to speak. Even though he was an observer with no voting power, Arthur was still an important guest. Graciously, he commended the presentation. His kind words, while welcome, had a perfunctory tone, which induced dread about what might be coming next. He then dropped this little bomb: "I must say, in all candor, that we would be crazy to invest more money in this company. From what I understand, it has failed to turn a profit with the business it has."

He paused, and there was a distinct sense of more to come. He looked around the room and made eye contact with the board members, passing over us as if we were invisible or irrelevant.

"Look, you gave them time to develop other strategies, which did not materialize. Now they return with a retail strategy when they have no retail experience and no merchants on board."

Damn. In fairness, as I sat silently, I knew I couldn't deny that his points were reasonable. I sensed, too, that he was flexing muscle from his new roost, and I felt personally challenged. Regardless, this was no time to indulge my insecurities. While his words hung in the air for what seemed like much longer than a few seconds, heads around the room turned to me with newly doubting eyes. In that moment, I felt I had morphed into a mature, grown-up woman who could handle this with confidence and grace. I was present and whole.

I responded: "Arthur, thanks for your candor. Everything you say is correct. I can't quarrel. I think it is important to keep in mind that Gymboree is more than a particular product or service. We are a household brand that *transcends* any particular product or service. While we have instant name recognition, we also have a brand that instills people with a warm and reassuring feeling about children, family, and life in general. When the public sees our name, it experiences something more profound and deeper than a play center. Gymboree means inclusion and connection. This cannot be overestimated. As you know better than I from your time in the industry, Arthur, history shows that household brands, like Weight Watchers for example, have a unique ability to expand well beyond original concepts, services, or products. We are positioned to take our place in that history. Despite our setbacks—perhaps because of them—we are ready to break through in a big way."

I stated, too, that while our current team could handle an initial store, we had money in the plan to retain any needed expertise. I added that seasoned retailers could be recruited once we proved the concept and rolled out. I closed: "It makes sense to show you what we can do and then bring on seasoned talent as needed. One store is within our grasp and capability. We are ready. Believe in this company the way we do."

I scanned the room, making eye contact with board members as I delivered my final words.

"This, everyone, is our time."

The smiles reappeared. All of the board members and investors wanted to believe that Gymboree was a winner and their investments would pay off.

Stuart Moldaw inserted himself: "I have spoken to Joan and the team, and, if we decide on a trial run, we can work with them for what is needed for a pilot store. I believe we see all the points and perspectives. The plan we have before us is quite complete for our study. Best we let this rest for today and think it over, and take everything into consideration."

The meeting ended on this ambiguous note. I had hoped for resolution at the meeting, yet I realized that would be unrealistic given everything the board had to digest, including the Hasbro deal going south. We stayed positive and braced for days of wait, hope, and see.

The next day Stuart called me.

"Joan, it's Stu. Really good job yesterday. Look, I believe in you; I always have. The board does too and has given you the green light. Go to Hong Kong and produce your line, and when you return, find a retail location, and we will open a store. If it goes like I think it will, we will raise the money and be back in business." USVP and Montgomery anted up $500,000 to get us started.

I was emboldened. Rugged entrepreneur or not, having my mentor believe in and stand by me was reaffirming. Through his supportive words, I felt more connected to our team and our purpose. Whether this boost would yield the ultimate win was anyone's guess. We took comfort knowing that we were still in play. Next up, Hong Kong.

CHAPTER 11

The Power in the Possible

LESS THAN A WEEK after the green light cleared us for apparel production in Hong Kong, the Gymboree family gave Julie and me a roaring send-off to the Asian continent. The anticipatory optimism was so heartwarming. I cherished getting another chance and appreciated how close to collapse we had come. After enduring the Hasbro incident, on top of our licensing program going nowhere, I would have understood if the board had directed us to break camp and focus on a write-down exit strategy. I didn't dwell on this possibility, but it was a reality check that underscored my gratitude. My relief reached beyond the business. Bill was now with a start-up public relations and lobbying firm, and it would be several months before he saw a steady salary. If Gymboree had crashed, wiping out my income, we'd have been hung out to dry.

And so we were off to Hong Kong to produce our kid's apparel line. Crammed into a literal back-row United supersaver coach section, Julie and I imagined ourselves on a space shuttle mission. Having only cross-country domestic flights for comparison, the trip seemed interminable. Curling up like cats, one of us on our seats and the other on the floor right below, we tried to sleep. No such luck. Too pumped, I guess.

During the flight, with shuteye not an option, we reviewed our mock-ups repeatedly. The details were measured out to the proverbial T. Real-life Gymboree kids had served as fit models. The exact colors had been preselected from fans or wheels familiar to us from home paint-chip samples. I was super-anxious and wanted to be ready for action upon arrival at the production facilities. We had to finish production in record time and get a store open before the major holiday retail season. No matter that we had no store location yet, and it was already May! An exhilarating freedom came with this taking-the-plunge feeling. It's a wonderful sensation when you're building a business.

In Hong Kong, people were everywhere, the pace brisk and the energy frenetic. New York on steroids! The unique landscape was a vivid confluence of seemingly haphazard high-rises and breathtaking bamboo scaffolding. I was worried my naiveté was apparent. It was time to don my grade-A unfazed and faux-sophisticated persona. I repressed my wide-eyed gaping so everyone would assume I was more experienced and this was business as usual. Good thing I had my well-honed "act as if you belong" behavior to call up on cue.

Julie's husband, George Arvan, was Gap's senior VP of merchandising, and he'd used his connections to get us a top-shelf factory producer, Li & Fong. Their production team met us on arrival. This was my strong suit; I was always at ease meeting new people. Being courteous and inquisitive flowed naturally from my mannerly upbringing. I enjoyed it, too. Julie and I visited more than a dozen factories after running through our entire line with the Li & Fong folks. We were on the go nonstop.

Bad news. Despite the endorsement of Li & Fong, our product runs were too small to meet the barest required minimums. No factory would accommodate us. The inevitable conclusion: we had to produce literally twice what we needed (and what made reasonable sense) for our store opening in order to satisfy their production minimums. Ugh. We came back to earth.

I called Stuart. How much more bad news could I deliver and still expect help? After listening to my report without asking a single question, he responded, in no-brainer style, "OK, produce the required minimums and we will open two stores." *Huh?* I don't know what I had imagined, but I was incredulous he would be that game. Stu was well into his 50s at that point. While I never asked him why he was so willing to take such a flyer with so much riding on the landing, my guess is that Stu, despite his crusty exterior, had set aside a small place inside for Peter Pan to take up occasional residence. He was special—and he believed.

Amazed, Julie and I went from preparing for the ultimate bad

news to having the stakes doubled! The reaffirmation acceler-
ated our momentum for the retail trial run. Retail portended a
new lease on life. How does it go—the only thing you can change
is yourself? Well, that was what we did. Each key player at Gymboree had an upward attitude adjustment. The confidence of the
board was rising. Just a few weeks earlier, Gymboree had faced a
Humpty Dumpty moment. But I had little time to muse. We had
much work to do.

We returned to California after less than a week in Hong
Kong. The production process commenced with urgency. Julie
was responsible for making sure our unisex product line worked.
She reviewed the arriving samples, the color runs, and everything
else from inception to final product delivery. Nancy Bott under-
took the back-office functions, including choosing cash registers
and computers, setting up payroll and permits, and arranging
the financing. Linda Rasmussen handled recruiting and hiring—
she already essentially ran our franchise operations. Mykie Rydal
and Sue Alley ran the first two stores. (Mykie, some 30 years later,
is still with Gymboree, now on the franchise side.) Bud Jacob at
first straddled roles as director of franchise development and
head of retail real estate, and eventually changed over to the
latter. The leases, lawyers, contractors, and mall personnel were
all going full throttle. Karen Anderson readied for press, product
placements, and all the media interest I was sure would come.

Of course, eventually we would devise a strategy for substantial cross-promotions between the retail operations and the play
centers, to invoke a feeling of fraternal twins more than disparate

divisions. Our vision was that the two businesses would be glued at the hip under the banner of a unifying family brand. It was our special corner in the marketplace. To be sure, no children's retailer but Gymboree would be able to claim a play program that literally thousands of children and parents attended regularly. But for now, we weren't quite ready to let our Zees know about the retail launch. None of that could happen until we had found two well-situated storefronts, and that was my next chief task. It was almost June, and we had merchandise arriving soon for two stores we hoped would open right after Thanksgiving. I reached out to top malls in the region to make presentations for retail space. As luck (that essential success ingredient) had it, Valley Fair Mall was just opening in central San Jose. This mall location was ideal, surrounded as it was by four long-standing Gymboree play centers. Nordstrom and Macy's would anchor the mall and some top national shops had already signed leases. It would be the first true upscale mall to enter Silicon Valley. This mall could cherry-pick the best of the best, and I wanted to be there. I couldn't be defensive about our lack of a track record for even a moment, or feel the least unworthy because we were arriving so late to the party.

I got a meeting with the mall leasing agent and a representative of its management. They were gracious and interested in our story. I focused on how our presence would spawn overall success at the mall. I recycled my board story about how a Gymboree store would attract upscale customers to the mall, particularly at desirable morning hours. I regaled them with the BBDO research and talked about our brand history. I flooded them with press clips and storyboards. I reiterated that our presence would shower benefits on their other lease tenants and put money in their pockets.

The reception was positive. A few days later, Valley Fair offered us a slightly off-center-court location, sweetening the deal with build-out dollars to help defray our costs. The rent was in line, too. Each board member called me personally with enthusiastic congratulations. Trying to make more hay while the bright sun was shining, I negotiated a second lease in the San Mateo Hillsdale shopping center, where Macy's and Sears held the anchor positions. San Mateo, you will recall, had welcomed the first Gymboree play center six years prior, and now several others dotted the nearby landscape. We were center court at Hillsdale as well, with good rent, albeit no build-out dollars. It was a smaller store, though, so our build-out costs would be less. All good: great, in fact. This mall was just fifteen minutes from our home office. Bud worked with local contractors to ensure the construction could finish on time and on budget. We were meticulous with spreadsheet updates and daily task-by-task reviews created by the responsible staffers. Each puzzle piece had to fit: leases, staffing, build-out, and merchandise. This was our most refined and complete collaboration to date.

The plan was to open two Gymboree stores on traditional Black Friday, the day after Thanksgiving, 1986. This was a mere seven months after Hasbro walked on us and, by all indications, Gymboree's curtain should have fallen and been bolted to the floor. Whenever I need a reminder lesson in possibilities, I can recall this moment.

Come late November 1986, it was time to watch it all come together. Our shipments were off-loaded in Oakland and de-livered to our makeshift warehouse in Burlingame, where they were checked for quantity and quality before being moved to the store shelves a few days later, a super-tight schedule. Our in-store stockrooms were tiny, and as we sold down, our plan was to deliver more merchandise via our personal automobiles. We were still a year away from having a sophisticated computer auto-replenish-ment system, which essentially tracks the flow of products, spec-ifies replenishment needs, and, importantly, identifies inventory for sale by what is customarily called SKU (stock-keeping unit). At the time, our old-school method of "hand count what is on the shelves and bring more goods when needed" would have to do.

We stormed out of the gate with knit, cotton terry, and fleece fabrics that were great for kids to wear while playing. We carried only primary colors. We had nothing in woven fabrics, which we thought looked like grown-up clothes scaled down to toddler sizes. Everything had three-inch growth cuffs both at the ankles and wrists to enable longer wear than the traditional three-month maximum for most infant/toddler apparel. We had only solids—not from choice, as this too was a limitation due to our produc-tion quantities—which turned out to work in our favor because prints tend to go boy or girl. Solids speak unisex more strongly. All of this was fitting—pardon the pun—especially since we had no fitting rooms, one thing not needed for babies and toddlers.

So, there we were, on Thanksgiving, dodging the last of the store construction crews still installing lights and fixtures and finishing the customary punch lists in both locations. The POS (point of sale) equipment was being tested and techies roamed about to solve maiden-voyage bugs before the opening. The full complement of Gymboree personnel was working at one or the other of the two stores deep into the night, some of us until as late as 4:00 a.m., facing a store opening five hours away. We expected the mall to teem with people at 9:00 a.m. and we were committed to being ready. Both stores looked precisely like what we had initially imagined.

Friday, crowds lined up outside the doors like the ones salivating to buy iPhones some 30 years later. Strollers were everywhere, almost blocking traffic on our side of the mall. The cross promotion with the local franchise play centers had generated lots of action. The local press was there to cover our grand openings. The mall bosses were stunned at the energy and numbers we generated. Our pitch was true as billed—we could bring in the moms! Our sales were kite-high, and this continued past Black Friday, throughout the holiday season, and up to the end of January. We did $1,000 and $900 respectively per square foot in the two stores (1,000 square feet at Valley Fair and 800 square feet at San Mateo), which were mall records that year. We never imagined that our simple unisex line, sold only in solid colors, with no graphics or patterns, could set the benchmark by which malls measured their retailers. Gymboree even aced the veteran jewelry stores that typically outperform everyone because of their high-ticket, big-volume sales in small spaces. Word traveled far and wide. Soon our telephones rang with invitations to meet with major shopping-center developers.

Sometimes, lemons become lemonade. That was how it went for us. Our very "narrow and deep" (as it was called in retail lingo) merchandising strategy established a solid marketing platform for Gymboree. Customers knew what we stood for, and the media was piqued by our unique unisex, play-geared designs. The store design for the Valley Fair store won the prestigious ICSC (International Council of Shopping Centers) award for outstanding achievement in USA retail design for a new store less than 6,000 square feet. Does it get better than that for a new retail launch? Oh yes—our concern that the franchisees might fear relegation to second-fiddle status was allayed, as the Zees became excited once they saw how the cross-marketing programs infused their businesses. They felt invigorated too.

This was a pivotal period in Gymboree history. We created a fresh market niche in a crowded retail world, delivered on a promised new direction, layered it cohesively onto the foundation of our culture, and maintained a unified family brand. It was early, I knew, but I was jubilant, energized, and intoxicated with purpose. I wanted this high to last.

Along the way, I reclaimed much of my prior sense of invincibility.

I was tempted to dismiss my earlier doubts as fleeting nightmares, but deep down I knew better. I still hid my discomfiting moments, especially when I thought about the future. I harbored a desire to rewind back to the years when challenges felt within my grasp, and when my vision and leadership seemed whole and distinctly inseparable from Gymboree itself. Now, as our strategy took hold, I feared being separated from the company and myself, even though the team looked up to me and expected me to carry the mantles of leader and spokeswoman. The bigger Gymboree became, the more I lost my ability to dodge shadows, even though I continued to function well. Gymboree thrived, and as my rivulet of internal dissonance formed, I suspected it had to do with my real limits. Or, maybe, my real preferences. Either way, even as this awareness grew in me, I was still unwilling to look at it too closely or gain a deeper understanding of it.

The company's platform was expanding in ways beyond what I could picture, and I had counted all along on my vision to guide me. I knew the company was in a great place. Success—or perhaps what success would mean in order for me to lead the company all the way there, wherever that was—seemed both thrilling *and* unmanageable. I marveled that I had brought us as far as I had. Time and again, I did my best to suppress those more-than-fleeting feelings in favor of savoring the sheer joy of what we were accomplishing.

And while the ride felt glorious, I feared privately that this wild bronco would toss me to an unknown and scary fate. Most of the time, I could barely face these fears, let alone share them with anyone else. I refused to consider when this all might come crashing down, despite my escalating sense that what was happening at Gymboree would swallow me whole.

Mostly, though, I ran from myself because I was too overwhelmed and naive to know how to handle such complexities. Worse yet, I told myself, as Grandma used to tell me when I was a worried child, "The future will take care of itself and things will work out—they always do." I knew her salve was myth even then, but I had yet to develop better coping skills, since typically something would grab and divert my attention before I could sort those kinds of things out. So for now, I awaited the next lifeline.

CHAPTER 12

~~~~~~~~~~~~~~~~~~~~~~~~~~~~~~~~

The Secret Sauce

THE RETAIL LAUNCH incited a frenzy of new investor interest. Our astute board investors converted their earlier debt instrument to equity at the current stock price as they anticipated a surge in value from new money jumping into the capital pool. Several big-time East Coast financial firms requested personal road shows.

We hustled to assemble an improved, investor-friendly two-year store rollout plan that built on what we had presented at the recent board meeting. *Yeah, that should be easy*, I joked to myself. After all, we were now awash in experience after a whopping four months of performance—uniquely positioned to trot out refinements *far* more predictive of a future bottom line for investor digestion. Sarcasm aside, we understood that this was a moment on which to capitalize.

As we geared up to develop our pitch to interested next-round investors, Stuart insisted that the numbers "re-sound the bell," as he liked to put it. He cajoled, "Just get those retail numbers right and make them sing," a familiar refrain. The initial focus was to identify the specific malls in our geographic expansion target markets. Next, we tightened up the organizational chart, identified ripe spots for new major hires, and highlighted posts for the sorts of seasoned retailers whose absence had initially spooked Arthur Fremlin. Notwithstanding our limited experience, we projected anticipated costs for build-outs and got a handle on revenue predictions by studying our inventory dollars and merchandise planning costs. When shaken and stirred, we hoped the blended concoction would produce a darn good bottom-line reading on which we could deliver.

Amid the investor bustle, I enrolled in a unique B-school master's program a stone's fling from the Stanford campus. Professor Stuart Moldaw, he of the school of hard knocks, would meet with me after his tennis game on some Saturdays at his office on Sand Hill Road, home to the heavyweight venture capital firms. Stuart instructed through immersion and anecdotes rather than classroom case studies. On these weekends, I geared up for a one-on-one lesson with the Adidas-clad professor. I heard more than one casual courtside lecture on ground-game techniques for a Gymboree retail win. He possessed a quick-trigger mind and issued rapid-fire strategic bullets, brilliant and sans syllabus.

While generous with know-how, Stuart was not patient. That was fine, as I was not particularly patient either and fancied myself a quick study. (Well, qualify that—maybe only when I was interested.) Plus, his flattery and encouragement flooded me with natural antibodies against my virulent insecurities. Some of us improve with a tough coach; others, like me, blossom with constant and heartfelt affirmation. I wanted nothing more than to make good on the investors' money and vindicate their belief in me, especially that of my able mentor.

In anticipation that Gymboree retail might go gangbusters, Stuart taught me life lessons that went far beyond inventory and replenishments, fabrics and dye lots, production and factors, bank debt versus equity, incentive stock option plans, sophisticated financing techniques, and leasing. I marveled at his passion for his industry and saw how you can stitch wisdom into the pocket of any endeavor, even the making of clothing.

Then, Saturday School with Stuart took a sharp turn. As we gathered for a session following the retail launch, Stuart recounted how USVP had a penchant for plucking proven retail talent from existing entities and persuading them to implement visionary concepts that USVP had home-grown. In this way, USVP culled and assembled teams to develop what it envisioned as untapped slots in the marketplace. It was a compelling strategy: cherry-pick experts and persuade them to give life to the investment banker's visions, using the lure of stock plus salary. But a winning team, he lectured, can't survive without charismatic leadership, what he called the "secret sauce." Mostly, he continued, this comes prepackaged in passionate entrepreneurs. B-schools can only re-count and highlight the stories of such individuals. No quantum of analyzed case studies can impart the power and uniqueness of personality. Stuart was adamant that I was one of those singular leaders. He emphasized the vital importance of a strong back of the house that "the best B-schools can produce," but insisted that a CEO—"a real leader, like you"—need only be conversant and comfortable with the general concepts, and need not be an A stu-dent in operational ways and means.

I steadied myself, sensing he was not finished. My role, he stressed, was to remain visible, to "stay in the spotlight," he chuckled, "and keep everyone smitten with you. No one can re-place you, Joan. Your presence ensures that the heart of Gymbo-ree stays true as we grow." This smelled a little fishy, and I sniffed danger in the forthcoming details. I nodded: OK.

The buried lede was next. Stuart moved to his leather sofa, his body language setting a different tone, as he usually paced as he spoke. The Adidas sneakers flashed as he deliberately crossed his legs and said, "I have a VP of operations who is perfect for us and a terrific fit." His favorite word, *terrific*, at this moment did not sound terribly terrific. "We will need him on our org chart to show depth, as we hope to have a scale that justifies hiring his expertise now. Your highest and best use at this juncture is to inspire the field and the press. I cannot emphasize that enough; your talents are rare. We must capitalize on them."

This was not a question or debate invitation. This was "FYI." He was working me. I felt perspiration on my neck. My face flushed. Both were familiar from childhood as signs of shame. Was I failing my ad hoc MBA? Was I not good enough? Unsure, and with a gulp, I blurted, "Stuart, are you saying you are disappointed that I cannot handle operations?"

Smiling in that patronizing way a parent does with a child, he got up and walked over to where I was sitting in his plaid armchair, legs folded under me, and said in a fatherly way, "Joan, you are terrific!" (That goddamn word again.) "I wish there were more of you, really I do. I tell my daughters and Phyllis [his wife] how great you are all the time. No, Bill Nandor, the man I have in mind for VP of operations, is a no-nonsense, get-it-done kind of guy, and you are the rainmaker. Gymboree needs you out front. Trust me here, please."

I wanted this to work out. I knew he knew best and that bullshit was not his modus operandi. We shared a closeness formed in the early stages of building the company together, and this closeness had an aspect of love to it. Not romantic or family love, but rather a love that blended respect, fondness, and affinity. Still, that particular Saturday School with Stuart created a discernible shift in our relationship. I knew we were in a business relationship, first and foremost—an understanding that made me wiser.

I knew too that he believed in Gymboree, and in me. In truth, I had feared for some time that this day would come. *Fearing* the day and *living* the day, however, were different. While I understood and even accepted this new direction as best for the company, I was sad. I had to concede my operational limitations. The truth, however fair, can be difficult to digest. Someday, I feared, it would make little sense for me to lead the company, and I might devolve to mere figurehead. But it was time to flush these worries about the future and focus on what was right in front of me.

And, with that, a new era was launched.

So, Gymboree and I turned the page. Bill Nandor joined Gymboree as a rare male in our female-dominated company. To his credit, Bill took to his post with alacrity. A veteran retail operations professional, he didn't need much direction. Our male ensemble was no longer limited to Bud Jacob and Bob Campbell, the last men standing since the departures of two others (Sam Williams and Bruce Pederson) in the layoffs. Bud and Bob fit in well. Power trips and non-collaborative working styles wouldn't fly at Gymboree.

With Bill Nandor on board, we finished the new business plan. Stuart scrutinized the numbers and liked what he saw. Without fanfare, he trotted us out to do serial dog-and-pony shows for several pre-vetted venture funds. Stuart delivered the details on each group a day in advance of our presentation. He assured me I would be too distracted if I got bogged down trying to learn all of the company dynamics and personalities prior to the meetings, despite knowing how prepared I liked to be. He assuaged me by saying that my "innate ebullience, crackerjack understanding of the business, and passion for Gymboree" would be more than enough, knowing I would be more compliant and accepting with this sort of boost.

We spread our presentations over the course of a few days, running them back-to-back. The schedule was grueling. Like a Broadway show, our little cast—Julie Arvan, Bill Nandor, and me in the lead—performed one or two times a day for a week straight. Like countless aspiring entrepreneurs, our fragile hope was that someone would "show me the money." Stuart reassured me that once one committed, others would follow.

He called it. The first dime to drop was the Harvard Endowment Fund, and I could not have been happier. For one, I liked Michael Eisenson, the fund manager, and the inclusion of Gymboree in the venture arm of the school's investment portfolio was a feather in our cap. As predicted, once this news got out, venture firms inundated Stuart with their interest. He was the one who decided who got in on the investment and how much stock each could acquire. The pricing held firm. USVP and Montgomery enjoyed a nice spike in their initial investment, as we priced the new monies substantially higher than their cost bases. There was, however, a catch: all of the stockholders pre–new money, including me and the ISO (the incentive stock option plan I initiated), would suffer dilution. And while the new money came at a higher valuation, which lessened the impact of dilution, and while the current venture investors would be diluted too, the board created a new preferred stock category for all investors, prior and new. Thus, in the future when a "liquidity event," such as acquisition or an IPO occurred, preferred stockholders would enjoy priority on distributable funds, while we common stockholders would have to wait in line behind them to realize upside with any remaining funds.

Stuart's characteristic response: "Do you prefer a little piece of a big pie or a big piece of a little pie worth relatively little?"

The new investment translated to $6 million in fresh funds for our retail rollout. We were transformed, and the company was about to change dramatically. I wondered about a shorter executive management leash, reduced decision-making autonomy, and lower investor and board tolerance. More success meant more scrutiny and a higher bar for performance.

New investor arrivals also meant a reconstituted board, as the newbies, except Chemical Bank, wanted a chair at the board table. None, thankfully, made board placement an investment contingency. We wanted a manageable board size. Even though Chuck Bernstein and George Gaber stepped down to make room, we still couldn't accommodate all the new players. The board pillars remained: Stuart of USVP, Linda of Montgomery, and me. We added Nancy Glaser, another USVP partner; new investors Dale Vogel from Norwest Venture Partners and Art Berliner from Walden Venture Capital; and our new CFO hire, Jim Higgins.

I now had to make monthly presentations to the board on a wide array of subjects, including the financials. Preview packets with finite results went out before each meeting. I walked members through the packets like a seasoned pro, and surprised myself with how quickly I navigated the steep learning curve and made sense of the numbers. I could see the storyline hidden in the P&L. I swung between feeling in command and out of my element. In fairness to myself, I was growing weekly. My optimism modestly outpaced my earlier sense that I was in over my head, at least in the current circumstances. Early on, by contrast, I had often felt I was faking it, a fraud. Now, I could better understand the powerful disincentives for learning on the job that can torment entrepreneurs.

Replicating our winning store formula felt doable. Fortified by my reliable instincts, we moved forward robustly. We opened more stores in the San Francisco Bay Area and made our way to the East Coast. Bud Jacob shifted seamlessly from franchise sales to store development. His vast experience with site location and leasing made him a natural. He groomed our franchise quality assurance guy, Bob Campbell, as his protégé handling domestic and international franchise development. Bob was charismatic, and he had been not much more than 25 or so when he joined Gymboree. He had a natural charm and the franchisees he supported adored him. Bob reported to franchise VP Linda Rasmussen, developing new franchise territories and building international markets. He grew and continued to impress, and earned the title of president of the franchise division in the years that followed. Julie Arvan was our super creative, a veritable one-woman band. Once a week, she showed us new styles planned for Hong Kong production in anticipation of the upcoming season. The management team, and of course anyone else around who wanted to chime in, were her built-in mother-in-law research. The fit models for our apparel sizing, ads, and catalogs were children of local employees or play program attendees. We were homespun to the core.

Growth was meteoric. Bill Nandor hired district, regional, and store managers. A true star was Muffet Moore, hired from one of Stuart's past companies. Brought out of retirement, Muffet became Gymboree's first regional manager and later catapulted to VP of store operations, a monster job that ultimately involved overseeing several hundred stores. A magnetic personality, Muffet was immortalized in Gymboree culture. One annual report quoted her prominently above an illustration of the team: "Our customers are loyal, yet they expect a great deal from our people and our product. So to succeed, we have to truly focus on exceeding their expectations every day."

Bill set the overall tone in this era. He spent time with each store, reviewing performance and comparing neighboring stores and mall averages. He was bursting with useful reports and insights. I asked him to present to staff in order to educate all of us on the new business, demonstrate our commitment to the rapid growth of the retail enterprise, and enhance our confidence in him. The team appreciated the opportunity, knowing I usually reserved reports that showcased top-notch staff for the board. This also underscored my general aversion to micromanaging employees. The company was only as good as the sum of its parts. It made no sense for me to shadow anyone.

My vision for board presentations involved a theatrical element. Rehearsals were required and roles refined. Not surprisingly, Bill Nandor's maiden voyage with the board was a grand slam. They praised him, Stuart beamed, and I was proud. Confidence filled the room. From Bill's entry on the scene, the board tracked his ability to deliver. When Stuart wanted to promote Bill to senior VP of operations, I was game. It all made sense, and I felt no threat. I liked that so many posts reported to Bill in the organizational chart—although I was well aware "the buck stopped" with me. I had plenty to do. I oversaw all aspects of the franchise business, retail merchandising, the CFO, marketing, and public relations. I was on the road often, solo, going wherever S&S Public Relations and Karen Anderson sent me. I had a rigorous interview and TV appearance schedule. The investors were proud and happy.

Despite our shortfall for a quarter or two, we received a full vote of confidence for a subsequent round of expansion. By the summer of 1988, we had 13 retail stores and board approval to open 20 additional retail stores in the next year, and more the year after that. This meant that in a mere three years, we would go from zero to nearly 40 retail stores. During a Saturday School with Stuart session, Professor Moldaw gave the go-ahead to plan "as if," driving a vision for a 120-store chain, which the board also later approved.

Meanwhile, the timing of our new retail hires dovetailed with the expiration of our corporate office lease. We began work on a new lease for major new headquarters. Once we moved into our exquisite new Gymboree offices in 1988, my personal pressure valve reset to my usual simmer. Less than a mile away, our new home had a tonier feel while still exuding Gymboree casual. The receptionist station mimicked our retail payment counter— the "cash wrap"—rounded and red with our primary-colored dancing Gymboree logo letters adorning the front in warm maple wood. While the building was modern and austere, our offices sat on the fourth floor and had beautiful bay views. Next to our entrance sat a gallery showcasing framed press clippings. Three times as big as before, the offices housed a design studio for the retail operation and war rooms where maps hung to show growth plans for both play and retail.

The company's family feeling kept us rooted as we shifted focus toward a business that was different from our initial reason for being. We remained heartfelt in everything we did and believed that, even as a retailer, our interaction with store customers was another golden thread in the fabric of our play-center philosophy. The integral aspects of our retail foundation—fun, playful, upbeat, colorful, and respectful of what works best for kids—mirrored what defined the franchise business and fueled the original play centers. We were now an integrated network of franchised play programs and company-owned retail stores. We always tried to articulate this self-description in one breath to showcase that the businesses were joined in harmony.

As the first retail year drew to a close, Gymboree was becoming a commercial force. The malls continued to court us despite a dearth of substantial retail history. We were no longer a stepchild in the USVP portfolio. Each week investors called me for personal updates. They loved the one-on-one connection. So did I, though I did misread these interactions as fledgling friendships rather than the strictly business relationships they were. Still, I enjoyed this personal interaction immensely.

I could barely catch my breath. Nor could I shake the burgeoning sense that our startling growth meant the business was outgrowing me, even though no one said so. The admiration of the media and the respect of my high-powered board felt like a riptide. My talents lived in the creative and visionary processes and the launch phase of business building. The nuts and bolts of expansion neither suited nor particularly interested me. I loved creating. I was passionate about innovation. The rest? Well, in truth, others were more skilled than I at most everything, except maybe when it came to being the icon for the company, and even that I found debatable. Part of me, though, still yearned to wrap my hands around the entire company as I had in its nascent years. I was conflicted.

While I was still the face of the company, I was no longer regularly in the trenches. The more we expanded, the more different roles were allocated to others. I no longer felt indispensable; I was coming to grips with my corporate mortality. I tried to remind myself, "Job well done. You built a brand, something that will outlive you." That, and not personal legacy, was the ultimate goal, I reminded myself: brand building. *Gymboree*. Right. And so the blurry writing on the wall foreshadowed that my days as the leader of Gymboree might be numbered.

And as my once-omnipotent grip on "my" company loosened, my eating disorder resurfaced inexorably. I was becoming less sure I could keep my struggles submerged. My behavioral tendencies kept pace with the escalated business tempo, increasing the risk of implosion. My internal voices became more disordered. My sense of instability grew, despite or perhaps because of the huge business success. Manageable can become unmanageable in different ways, but usually the coup is gradual and unceremonious, if no less formidable. My bulimia was no fair-weather visitor. It advanced at a clip that outpaced Mom's admonition to keep up a "good face," especially on those dark days when I knelt over a toilet tossing my cookies undetected in the Gymboree offices, a violent enactment to purge my pain and confusion. Not every day was that troublesome, which made the whole thing more confounding. The next day I would vow to stop this disgusting nonsense. And I did—for a while—even as serious storms began to blacken the horizon.

CHAPTER 13

∞∞∞∞∞∞∞∞∞∞∞∞∞∞∞∞∞∞∞∞

Be a Fly on Your Own Wall

THE ASTONISHING SUCCESS of Gymboree did not bode well for everyone. Growth often means personnel changes, as the people who got you there can't necessarily continue to provide enough value to justify retention. As a matter of sound business sense, this seems inarguable, but what often makes rational sense in these circumstances can wreak havoc with our deeper sensibilities. And in my case, it did.

As we grew, I never considered the idea of an expiration date for any of our core group. The members of the Origin Team, as I came to call us, had stuck by the company with unconditional allegiance through all the highs and lows and inversions and curves, not to mention salary cuts. They never wavered from our mission or showed ambivalence about our ability to succeed. And, vitally, they consistently elevated the interests of the company above their own. We had been roped in the life raft together as we fought for survival, and each year had strengthened and toughened us to meet recurring challenges. Operating with mutual trust and respect, the Origin Team had built something special from the ground up. We lived according to an unspoken creed that we were all for one and one for all. The learning-on-the-job cliché seemed tame next to our naive bravado that we had gotten the company this far on chutzpah, heart, love, and, dare I say, loyalty. Yes, loyalty.

I was devastated when I began to realize that on this next battlefield, the major retail rollout, we needed different partners—and that this meant that some of our longtime comrades-in-arms would have to be, as the business lingo has it, "let go." My chronic personal dread, once limited to feelings of being in over my head, latched on to the company imperatives that called for "more efficient allocation of human resources." (If ever there was a euphemism . . . .)

The operational dilemma was this: as we imported new specialists, the initial staff, including me, redounded to generalist status. This made for a precarious position. The bell had rung for jacks-of-all-trades to surrender to people with specific expertise—even though, over the years, we had ably worn as many hats as the business required. One day I would be the marketing maven, the next day the financial wizard securing credit lines, and the next day the R&D expert focused on new product introductions.

Any member of the de facto generalist corps had held at least three jobs at different times, or even simultaneously. That was how we rolled in the early years.

I was not insensible of this new corporate reality. Still, I was too immobilized to deal. Was this weakness or strength? Was it so clear it had to be one or the other, or did my internal conundrum bespeak something more complex, more gray? I was being tested, big time, and I knew it. I had to figure out how to find the strength to fire members of my beloved team. And I couldn't even *imagine* doing it. Shit.

At first, in my time-honored way of coping, I hid my fear, just as I had when I was a girl. Back then, I hid many aspects of myself because of my longing for my mother's love. I would suppress my hurt feelings for fear that disclosing them would upset her. When I was teased or left out at school, Mom would just accuse me of doing something that invited the cruel actions of the other kids. No comfort—just a furrowed brow, with an accompanying projection of shame.

Now, as CEO with increasingly hefty responsibilities, I lacked the luxury of burying my head in the sand. I knew what had to happen but I struggled to act. Some days it felt like all-out war internally. My breath would go shallow and my blood pressure would drop to scary depths. On one occasion, Nancy Bott found me on the floor of my office in the throes of presumed heart failure or stroke, and had to drag me to a nearby emergency room. The diagnosis: panic attack. When that happened, I was transported back to that vexing day some fifteen years before, when, on being told of my first pregnancy, I was offered an opportunity to schedule an abortion. My tough, capable exterior masked a soft underbelly. The thought of letting go any of my inner circle, my Origin Team, struck me as a form of death.

So far as I could tell, only I knew that the days were numbered for some among us. The company was focused on the retail strategy: store build-outs, timely merchandise supply, collaborative cross-marketing with the franchisees, and more. I kept under wraps the inevitability of personnel cuts. The weight of the secret made it difficult, but during most daylight hours I was able to stay busy as usual. When I couldn't easily dismiss the impending reality, though, my eating disorder took over. The disorder progressed, a hostile march toward dominance. Intermittently, I had some extremely bad days, as the disease besieged me. When these hellish days came frequently enough, I began to pay more attention. I desperately clung to some sense of control. Then, a long string of many nightmarish days began to extend into months, when no distractions proved capable of numbing the pain.

This was my daily life at this juncture: I rose circa 5:30 a.m. and punched the button on the coffee pot prepared the night before. While the first caffeine fix brewed (I still thought of coffee as a relatively harmless vice), I skipped down the outdoor wooden steps in the morning darkness and into the damp basement laundry room. After starting a load of wash, my eyes might fix on a hamper containing a T-shirt we'd bought one of the kids in the Sierra. This would trigger a sense of happiness and security.

I would dutifully interrupt the comforting reminiscences to scurry upstairs as I remembered the long list of self-imposed to-dos I needed to check off before everyone awoke. After taking care of early domestic business, I might bike up Mount Tamalpais, as our home was snuggled at its base. Mountain biking fed my exercise jones. Or I might take a run up the mountain. Or hit an early high-impact aerobics class. In any and all cases, this happened while my family slumbered.

After the various early a.m. fixes, I returned to prepare the kids' lunches, finish the laundry, get ready for work, and have breakfast with the family. I left about 8:00 a.m. with the girls in tow for school drop-off. I liked the exclusive "us" time in the morning, and though we had a live-in au pair during those years, she wouldn't really emerge until after the rest of us departed for the day. This allowed me to feel I was still filling a conventional mom role, even though the growth of Gymboree had reshaped what that meant. Little in how I mothered resembled anything I remembered as a child. I was now a very different young mom, both from my own mom and others of her generation, and from most other moms I knew at the time.

En route to our Burlingame office (a 45-minute commute), I stopped at a local café in Mill Valley to grab two lattes, which entered my system even before I arrived at the freeway entry ramp 10 minutes from my home. On days where the pressure seemed sky high, I stopped at another café right before entering the freeway for a third latte, and then detoured off the highway to buy a fourth before arriving at the office to start the workday.

Arriving at work around 8:45 a.m., flying high from the caffeine and what remained of my exercise endorphins, I made my rounds, visiting key personnel to see how I could support them. Few would have believed I was in the throes of a major internal crisis and not keeping it all together. I returned to my office, called a few key franchises, and checked the daily retail sales reports. I took a telephone call from a board member to discuss this and that, another from the press, and then handled other interviews that our PR agency had scheduled for me. Smile for the camera, please!

By late morning, my jitters would return in force, signaling a call for more exercise in order to regain composure. For this round, however, I corralled people from their offices—often over friendly objections, as they had work to do—for a grueling aerobics class I conducted to the sounds of a playlist I had created. The playlist production was fast becoming one of my favorite CEO tasks, intensifying the addictive satisfaction I found in the exercise. Most everyone accepted my "invitation" to avoid showing me disrespect. It was not lost on me, however, that in fact I was the one exhibiting disrespect by interrupting their workday. But I felt helpless to refrain, as I was captive to my exercise-addiction master.

Mostly, I ate lunch at my desk, which I followed with laxatives and (sometimes) purging to minimize the food's impact on my body. This meant that before too long I needed more food. Commonly, I felt light-headed and dizzy. Bulimia can wreak mayhem through its effect on blood sugar levels and blood pressure, not to mention tooth decay, damage to the digestive system, and other very serious health issues. Then there was the popcorn ritual, childlike and fun, befitting our culture; everyone got a kick out of the CEO toting a bowl of popcorn to her desk. The popcorn kernels were no mere snack; they substituted for an intravenous drip into my system to keep me from collapsing or getting frenetic. To everyone else, the routine had its charm. From the inside, though, the deceptions compounded my sickness.

Let me say at this point that food addiction is no day at the beach. Experts consider it one of the most difficult addictions from which to recover. At least with drugs and alcohol there is no negotiating: You use or you do not use. Food, however, cannot be avoided. Newer, healthier consumption patterns have to be established. Once caught under the addiction spell, making friends with food again for fuel and pleasure—and not for comfort, punishment, reward, or anger management, to name a few— can require a transformation.

My crazy days did not end at the office, which I typically left no later than 6:00 p.m. On the way home, I often hit another local exercise class. Arriving at the house, I sat with the kids as they ate the dinner the au pair had prepared. After I put them to bed, read stories, or played games, Bill and I typically headed out to dinner. When we returned, depending on the night, I might purge again. Sometimes I stayed amped deep into the night, unable to unwind and fall asleep. Many of those nights, I went for a nighttime run over a trail leading to the Pacific Ocean or along the San Francisco Bay, not another soul visible at that wee hour.

When I would fall asleep, nighttime was far from restorative. A frequent recurring nightmare would cut off my meager sleep in brutal fashion. Sometimes, the nightmare replayed later that same night. It went like this: I was living alone in a classic haunted house, through which I walked, alone and fearful, until I emerged on the back porch—only to see innumerable decapitated cats strewn across parched clay ground. No trees, no vegetation, just thirsty land littered with grotesque and brutal death on a cold earth.

Upon awakening, I was tormented and prayed this was not happening. Were the cats my colleagues? Who else could they be? And the haunted house? Did it represent what was becoming of my Gymboree family "home," a wellspring of agony?

That was my life. Ironically, I was functioning well during my workdays, and the media had lost no love for Gymboree. Many were fascinated with the CEO and her founder-led aerobics class, the healthy popcorn ritual snack, and the casual-Friday dress code every day. The clues to my impending crash were unwittingly glamorized.

I realized I needed time to think, away from Gymboree and my family. I hatched a plan. I was attracted to Native American traditions and sometimes participated in sweat lodges and similar rituals. I decided to enroll in a weeklong vision quest in early August 1988, held in the Sweetwater Mountains, a mountain range located in the high country overlapping the California and Nevada borders. A vision quest is a rite in some Native American traditions that entails spending a few days secluded in nature, fasting, sleeping under the stars, and seeking deep self-awareness through connection with natural forces and spiritual energies. My Sierra cabin was only a few hours away through the high country, and spending a couple more weeks there to integrate the weeklong vision quest ritual and find more balance and clarity seemed right. My daughters would be at sleepaway camp and Bill was plenty busy at work. I felt calmer already.

I couldn't imagine a bogeyman crossing the Sierra to penetrate my unconscious and find me in that pristine place along the American River. I hoped to tap into a wider vision for how to serve myself, help the company I had founded, and do right by my people. I knew few would understand this methodology—it was too new age (*The CEO is going where?*), not a strategic style likely to draw high-fives from venture capitalists, much less investors scrutinizing a major retail rollout a year after a big capital raise. It was, nonetheless, an expression of who I was, and I was committed to following my instincts where they led me.

I first satisfied myself that things would be fine with me gone. Bill Nandor handled all the store operations with great skill and Linda Rasmussen had everything under control on the franchise side. Reassured that the company was in excellent hands, I didn't ask for permission, however diplomatic that would have been. I simply announced I was taking the time off. Stuart got it and asked no questions.

What was in store for me beyond this mini-sabbatical? I had no clue. Nor did I have a personal agenda or goal. I was in the grips of tumultuous change, and there was no clarity ahead. Shades of Hasbro—only this time I was fighting for me, not the company.

CHAPTER 14

⬦⬦⬦⬦⬦⬦⬦⬦⬦⬦⬦⬦⬦⬦⬦⬦⬦⬦⬦⬦⬦⬦⬦⬦⬦⬦

It Would Not Be at Your Gate, Unless You Could Handle It

THE VISION QUEST and Cabin sojourns made for an uninter-rupted journey of honest introspection. Each day I faced myself with little distraction as I sought to discover what I wanted for myself apart from Gymboree. In the sagebrush, I felt courageous and resilient. When I made shelter with a tarp and rope in a summer thunderstorm on the solo phase of the vision quest, I felt self-reliant and without panic. I spent most of my time out-doors, the force and beauty of the natural world chipping away at the barriers to my inner knowing. I experienced the same sense of creativity and capability that had filled me back when I'd felt more secure as Gymboree's steward and CEO—although this journey was fundamentally different than what awaited me back at Gymboree. Yet the breadth of my experiences felt akin to an entrepreneurial endeavor, replete with its own brand of obstacles. To build is to build, be it a business or, in this case, my shelter. I was assembling a toolbox with which to reconstruct my foundation. To get there, I needed to discover my deepest wishes, and figure out how to put those first.

On the final night of the vision quest we were invited to perform a ritual involving the close people in our lives. I collected stones and used them to create a circle around myself, each representing an important relationship in my life. Sitting in the middle of my stone ring, I went around the circle and spoke aloud to these "people" as if they were present. While I was sharing my reveries, my regrets, and more, shooting stars streamed overhead. I took this as a signal that someday my life would have a more serene quality. My relationships were the cornerstones of my being, and they had lost their priority in my life. Yet, according to a saying I had learned from my study of indigenous cultures over the years, "It would not be at your gate, unless you could handle it."

I was aware that upon my return to Gymboree, I would continue to play my professional role and discharge my responsibilities, but (I hoped) with a different inner mind-set. I knew that good health and wholeness would not just appear gloriously after I returned, and that my month away wouldn't be an instant cure. The path ahead was fraught with daunting and invasive spade work.

During my time away, insulated from the pressure of the job, my relationship with food normalized. I easily gave up coffee and felt no urge to eat and purge—I only ate for sustenance. I imagined (or hoped) that past dysfunctions had lifted and taken leave. Nor had I felt any compulsion to exercise intensely. None of it. It was as if—for these weeks away—the hellish dual life of high-functioning entrepreneur and closet bulimic had been embodied in someone else. It did not occur to me during this respite that the unanswered siren calls of a gentler, less pressured lifestyle were at the core of my escalating eating disorder. During that month, I shed the past, lived in the present, and projected little into the future, including what awaited me at Gymboree. I powered down on all fronts. Soothed by the magic of the mountains, I trusted I would find my way when I returned, including some skillful, sensitive means of handling the inevitable layoffs of Origin Team members.

When I returned to Gymboree in September, Stuart invited me to his Sand Hill Road office. This was not a Saturday School makeup class but rather a no-nonsense weekday meeting. He explained that a few weeks earlier, at a board meeting held in my absence, the board members had resolutely latched on to what I had been dreading for months. The time had come to move out some of the "old-timers," as Stu uncharitably referred to them, and he wanted to identify who should be let go. Taking two deep breaths, I made a conscious decision to reserve all of my emotional reaction for later. For the time being, I had to be all business. We agreed to cut three key members of the Origin Team, as well as a few more who would be asked to depart over the next few months. We examined the nuts and bolts of the process, such as execution of stock options and outplacement planning for the affected people.

As hard as this was, the absence of any emotion coming from Stuart was disconcerting. He treated the whole affair as a perfunctory part of real-world decision-making, and dismissed the layoff process as mere "growing pains." When I realized this, I felt at once angry, confused, and disillusioned, and also sad that he seemed so lacking in compassion. I tried to persuade myself that his matter-of-fact demeanor was his way of shielding any internal discomfort. That much at least I could understand. Except, honestly, I didn't think this was the case. Perhaps he thought me more hardened because of the prior downsizing, or perhaps he wanted to protect me emotionally. Regardless, one thing was sure—there was no conversation that day about the hardships of growing a business.

My interaction with Stuart made me think of my childhood efforts to escape emotional suffocation. This time, I had no place to run. I needed to be adult and do my job. Not so easy. I knew that I had taken my sabbatical to steel myself for these moments, but that did not mean I would respond with detachment and seasoned aplomb. I needed more than the time away. In that moment, I needed to summon strength from deep within. I needed to breathe deeply, deep enough to land back inside myself, yet not in so obvious a way as to call attention to myself.

I forced myself to think, shift out of my onslaught of anger, fear, and distress. *OK, OK—maybe I go now, too.* Yes, maybe it was time for me to leave alongside the people I was going to fire. I was not cut out for this; I did not aspire to be that tough, as necessary as it might be. I transported myself back to my vision quest space and my recent time at the Cabin. I told myself: *You know where you are headed; do what you need to do. Gymboree needs what it needs. Your relationships with these people will find their way in the future; trust that. What you have forged with them lives on. Think beyond this moment.*

So, while the scared and self-righteous parts of me wanted to walk out on Stuart in that moment in protest, I rose with a straight back and said something like, "Thanks, Stu, for all you do for Gymboree and me. This is going to be hard and I'll take care of it. I understand it has to be done, and I am the one to do it." The voice I heard, mine, had strong resolve. It came from the part of me that understood duty and responsibility.

Thus, as 1989 was about to begin, we entered a time of endings at Gymboree. We replaced Julie Arvan, the sparkling merchant who had been the main architect of the retail strategy, with the seasoned and talented Nancy Pedot, who would become senior VP of merchandising and later the CEO who led the company into the public market in 1993. I said goodbye to Karen Anderson as well, as the company was no longer going to put money toward franchising and in-house public relations. The NEA column died with her departure. The inestimable Bud Jacob was walked out for a more seasoned real estate veteran, and we ushered in a whole department of folks to handle the rapid rollout and construction.

Nancy Bott brought me to the hospital yet again amid these firings, as I suffered a bout of vagus nerve pressure, which appears in the form of (but is not) a heart attack. Chalk it up to the heartbreak of the firings. To say this experience nearly killed me would not be hyperbole. Nancy survived the cuts and remained on staff for a few years longer, albeit reporting to controllers and people whose jobs were once hers. Linda Rasmussen stayed on several more years as the head of franchise operations. Bob Campbell, who had trained under Bud for franchise development when Bud got deployed into retail, was promoted to president of the franchise division. Also cut was the entire marketing department, decimated wholesale, as it was presumed I could carry that load.

Those who lost jobs in this wave were gracious—each a class act. Despite the inner voice suggesting that the ordeal would help me develop as a leader, this assignment was not a growth experience. Something shifted in me, and I was unclear whether I would be the same again. Some might have said the moment resembled a Zen koan, a paradox that cannot be resolved with reasoning and requires intuitive enlightenment to solve, while others—Stuart, perhaps—would have view it as just a garden-variety management task.

I returned to what had become the main question: Was it time for me to go too? Stuart kept saying that I exhibited leadership. But all the while I was being deafened by the clamor of debilitating inner voices. Where would I go if I left? What would I do? Was it easier to stay put in some capacity rather than confront what might lie ahead if I too were cut loose? The board kept showering me with accolades and the laudatory press interviews continued unabated. Everyone thought I was in control, and few suspected that the recent downsizing had taken such a toll on me. How could no one see how much I was struggling with the rapid growth and where I would fit in the expanded Gymboree? In fairness, I had managed to keep it pretty together on the outside despite the widening sinkhole inside. My earlier daily madness had subdued for the moment, aided by the month away. Yet I was concerned that a new tempest was brewing.

Meanwhile, my home life was slipping into disarray. I felt guilty about my almost-exclusive fixation on work throughout these years. If I was home, I worried I should be at work. If I was at work or traveling, I had pangs of guilt about not being home. My neglect of my husband and children as I focused on Gymboree and the brunt of my eating disorder had caused a fissure in our family. While I worked hard to attend to my children, I did not prioritize my marriage to the same extent I prioritized my company, and to complicate things, Bill was wrestling with his own issues. He and I seemed more distant together, and our communication less intimate. Even the lively banter about political issues of the day that once flowed so effortlessly between us had evaporated. Our hallmark of shared humor and laughter had become more the exception than the rule, and each week our conversations were increasingly pithy and remote. As I was prone to do when I sniffed danger, I focused elsewhere. After all, I rationalized, every long-term marriages endures ups and downs. I left it there.

By now, my kids were full-on teenagers, missing few of the predictable difficult stages that come with adolescence. There was no simple black and white here, only multiple shades of gray. I knew I could have been a better mother. Remarkably, though, both girls were excellent students, held jobs, and took part in numerous activities and sports; one was a talented artist and the other a talented writer. As so many kids do, they kept many of their feelings and experiences hidden from their mother. The mother ship, though, felt like it was capsizing.

Bill and I had been kids when we met, me 18 and he 21. It was quite a love affair. I met him in New York City on Thanksgiving vacation while we were in college, but we didn't really connect until a few months later, when I was skiing in Vermont. This was 1966. We started to date, but I insisted on maintaining my virginity, and we parted ways. But I never stopped thinking about him, and two years later, I looked him up in the phone book and called him. That very day, as serendipity had it, he'd returned from almost a year traveling through Central America, after he'd spent the 1967 "summer of love" in San Francisco. We picked up again and fell in love. It was the hippie era, and life was blissful. We married in the summer of 1969. I couldn't imagine life without Bill. It was easier to ponder life without Gymboree than life without my family, and unthinkable that I could lose both.

Bill decided he too wanted time on his own, as I had during the vision quest and Cabin interludes. I was agreeable, which was only fair, since he had been supportive of me taking time away. His "sabbatical," however, was to move out of our home and rent a local house, which made me uneasy and suspicious. While we wound up spending most of our time together, I was not sure what he was "figuring out," and did not ask. We still biked and spent time with the kids, who lived with me. Our lives were busy and full, just apart.

In the spring of 1990, I took on a new role at Gymboree. I was named chairman of the board, which I understood was a euphemism for being kicked upstairs. I was now out of all day-to-day operations. Bill Nandor, with my blessing, became president. I was fine with it. While I had dreaded this day for some time, I had readied myself for the eventuality. I was wearing down a little, too. The inevitability of change was apparent, and while I was accepting, I wanted no fanfare.

Meanwhile, Nancy Pedot was on fire. Stores opened faster than I could keep track. I attended openings as a ceremonial ribbon-cutter, or to offer a more substantial press interview. That much I did well. We kept opening stores, half in California and others sprinkled among D.C., Virginia, New York, New Jersey, Arizona, Miami, and Pennsylvania. Who could keep up? Stuart could. He stepped in as CEO, until he recruited Don Cohn to replace him, a hire the board approved near the fall of 1990.

Me, I barely held on. As my hopes for my marriage sank, so did the ground underneath me. At work, I was losing both momentum and desire, and I showed up less and less. My disorder behaviors were back with a vengeance. In particular, my exercise addiction peaked.

While preparing to compete in a highly competitive mountain bike race in the summer of 1990, I couldn't help noticing that my competitors were a decade or more my junior. The difficulty

of the race course unbalanced me from the start, and I was perplexed how I would survive one, let alone all, of the tortuous laps.
There were deep dirt climbs, water holes, steep rocky descents,
and turns with tricky sandy obstacles, each requiring substantial
technical skill. Plus, the course had a steep vertical ascent, which
was my weak spot. I reminded myself that slow and steady can
win a race. In this case, I was just hoping to finish!

I muffled the internal voices urging me not to compete, half
hoping I'd win and half hoping I'd crash. Rounding each lap, I
bargained with myself: if I just jumped the track, I could end the
pain. But I plowed ahead, even though I kept falling, shredding
my clothes and drawing blood. I don't remember much about
what happened at the end, but I learned later that the race over-
seers literally pulled me from the course and into the first-aid
tent. Sitting in that tent, bandaged, the tears welling, I had no
more fight in me. All the pushing stopped. Beat-up body, beat-
down spirit, tilt, game over. I was flattened, heartbroken, and lost
at 43.

CHAPTER 15

∞∞∞∞∞∞∞∞∞∞∞∞∞∞∞∞∞∞∞∞∞

Maybe to be Powerful is to be Fragile

"HI, I'M JOAN . . . I feel so exposed telling you all this."

I was at an AA meeting, a week after the bike-racing mishap, speaking both to everyone and no one. I rarely talked at these meetings despite having been a regular for over a year, when my awareness that I was struggling to stop my destructive behaviors (even though alcohol was not among them) had driven me to AA. My issues, as I understood things, were subsumed under what was called the "disease of addiction." It mattered not that my issues manifested in food, and others' in drugs, alcohol, gambling, sex, shopping, and so on. AA, the granddaddy of them all, offered the most frequent meetings and had the greatest recovery record. Many people in the rooms I visited had maintained 20, even 30 years of continuous sobriety. How inspiring—when, honestly, I could not string more than a few months together before trouble found me. I hoped I, too, could get cured in those rooms.

That day, I raised my hand, and when the leader called on me, I rose from the semicircle of seated addicts. Stammering some, more words came.

"Um, no, I did not slip. I did not drink or use drugs. I had a bad bike accident because I could not stop myself from competing in a race I had no business being in."

Good thing you didn't meet eyes at the fellowship when you spoke. Otherwise, I might have seen the "big deal, bike accident" puzzlement on many faces. After all, when people in these meetings rose to speak, they shared stories of serious relapses. My brand of addiction, replete with punishing workouts, seemed unworthy and trivial to me. Still, I knew after many months of AA experience that this room was a safe haven, regardless of what anyone had to say. In AA, there is no "cross-speak" or dialogue. You speak, and people listen. Simple.

Gaining my composure, I continued my confession, confident no one in the room would judge what I shared. I remained standing until my arms almost shook loose from my body. Finally, I managed a "thank you" and sat down.

I had convinced myself to attend AA meetings, acknowledging that I had some sort of "problem." But another part of me still downplayed that decision, reasoning that the anonymous and voluntary AA environment presented little risk and required no regular or long-term commitment. In addition, the meetings occurred in the mornings and on weekends, which allowed me to attend without telling Bill or my children (or anyone else). Besides, I rationalized, I really did not belong in a group populated by alcoholics. And I could walk away whenever it suited me. I was getting a lot out of it, mostly through learning about the benefits of a caring community dedicated to recovery with strength and hope. I liked being there. I eventually got a sponsor, and I had become a regular.

The day after my rare confession, my AA sponsor, Susan, invited me to hike. On the trail descent, she asked that we sit under an oak tree. She claimed she needed a respite from the bone-chilling fog and, besides, she had something to discuss, "eyeball to eyeball."

"Joan, it was good to hear you share yesterday in the meeting. I know that was hard for you. What I have to say, however, is that I, we, feel the fellowship may not be enough support for your recovery. Please know we fully appreciate that you are dedicated to becoming well and abstinent and do not drink or use recreational drugs; yet, your challenges with food and exercise are beyond the AA's scope."

She paused there for a reaction. The burning I felt inside defrosted the cold from the heavy fog. I unwound my scarf and removed my hat. My mind raced with fear and rushes of letdown: *Am I failing in recovery? Not living up to some timeline? Was there a timeline I was not told about? Is it because I am not drinking, doing recreational drugs, what? Why not hang with me? Don't you like me?*

She interrupted my train of concerns.

"Joan, you need a different type of help. We feel ill-equipped to give you what you need. I am recommending a place called Woodridge in Georgia that deals primarily with eating disorders."

I felt my head drop. I heard my heart thumping through layers of hiking clothing. I felt deflated and, worse, alone. Doubtless seeing the sad and resigned look on my face, Susan added: "Joan, I know this is hard. Eating disorders are tricky; Woodridge has a great reputation. I am sorry I cannot help you with this one."

It was bad enough I felt weak-willed; now I was abandoned. Not to mention that Georgia seemed as far away to me as the other side of the moon. Why was I was unable to stop these destructive behaviors? My laxative use and purging repulsed me. I was in the unyielding claws of an insidious pattern, with no sense of how to get free. Who cared that I looked normal, or worse, even "great," as I was told? Each morning as I kickstarted my resolve, bulimia beat me back down with ever greater frequency. I reflected on how I had felt that fateful afternoon in the first-aid tent, slumped and battered, covered in bandages, broken inside. I knew I had to take stronger action than sitting in AA meetings, only I wasn't sure what was best. I was certain that change was my only option.

It was September 1990, and Susan had named it. I needed to go to a treatment center. Something had shifted inexorably in that fateful Red Cross tent, as I bore warrior wounds from a war with myself absent a cause. Hardly a heroine, I began to see that I was lucky I was still alive. My willingness to attend AA meetings and forgo occasional and modest weekend wine or pot use was small when compared with the dark challenges of my core bulimia, which I had managed to elude for the whole year. My head-in-the-sand avoidance about my addiction was of a piece with the shame I felt about being in AA. I hid it all from my family. Only now can I see how I had tiptoed around my illness and avoided the road to recovery and the surrender I needed to get well. Eventually the expression "we are only as sick as our secrets" became understandable and painfully real to me, as that revealed to me the depth of my illness.

I gained sufficient clarity to vow that my addiction would no longer keep the upper hand, even though I was "functional" in the "real" world. My "acting as if" routines, and the enduring confidence that came my way via the endorsements of the board, Stuart, and the press, only stepped up the pressure. The folly of the bike race was both real and a metaphor for the true impending collapse. I hated being "sick," but I had finally realized that whatever it took to find my way to recovery, I had to find it. Yes, it would be difficult to tell Stuart and my team at Gymboree, not to mention my family, that I was off to a treatment center for 30 days. But I had no choice if I wanted to stay alive. As I went deeply inside of myself, I began to feel not only that I did not have a choice, but also that this was my choice, a choice that would bear out what I later learned addicts must change in order to recover: just one thing—*everything*.

I called the Woodbridge Clinic to get my 30-day program rolling. The admission folks were sensitive to the complexity of feelings involved in self-enrollment, which was the ideal. The soft-spoken lady from Woodbridge encouraged me to come immediately, within the next few days. In an instant, I thought *maybe I am not so bad*, the bargaining power of my addiction re-asserting itself: "Well, I have to take care of a bunch of stuff. I run a business and have two teenage daughters in high school. I will need some time to sort this all out." I considered changing my mind, my resolve fleeting. Yet I wanted, I needed, recovery. The interplay among these dynamics engaged all my shame, and all my resistance. The Woodbridge lady was a pro, though, and with her careful coaxing, I agreed to show up in five days.

I was no stranger to going into high gear when necessary. I was well aware of the impact this would have on my family. Each life piece, especially on the home front, had to be put in some form of order for me to make this move. So I did, one by one.

First, I called Bill to tell him I had decided to enter a 30-day residential treatment program in Georgia and I needed him to move "home" to be with the girls while I was gone. By now, of course, he was no stranger to my addictive patterns, though he—like me, until now—had never grasped the gravity of what I was experiencing. His first response was, "I understand what you are saying. I am curious if this is something you feel is necessary for you to do. It is a pretty major step." I assured him I had no choice if I wanted to get control of my life. He nodded thoughtfully and said little more. Although our marriage was unwinding, he was tender and supportive. Check.

I called Stuart and gave him the abridged story. Stu was supportive. He promised to "have my back" and cover for me with

the board, telling them I would be "away for personal reasons."
At the time, I was grateful for his empathy. In hindsight, though,
having him keep this secret wrapped my situation more securely
in shame. Either I believed it was shameful myself, or I did not
yet have the self-awareness to say it was fine to let everyone
know I was at a recovery center for bulimia.

I called my parents. They had only recently learned that Bill
and I were not living together, news I had suppressed because I
didn't have the nerve to tell them—covering, I think, in anticipation of my mom's feelings. To keep the charade going, every
Sunday during the separation, Bill and I had still called them together, our decades-old custom. When told of the separation, my
mom, not surprisingly, had come unglued at the searing news
that her daughter's "perfect" family had domestic woes. Now she
had to face the reality that her daughter had both marital problems and an eating disorder serious enough to compel entry into
a treatment center. Yikes. What would the bridge ladies think?
What would happen when her telephone no longer rang off the
hook with friends calling to announce they saw Joanie on the
Today Show or *CBS Morning News*?

Predictably, when I delivered the news about my impending
treatment, Mom first exclaimed how upset this made her. So
much for instinctive parental empathy. Then she tried to dis-
suade me from going, insisting my problem was "probably not
that bad." Piling insult on top of it all, she wanted to call Bill and
"get him" to return home so we could live as a reunited family.
Then all should be fine. I shuddered at her insensitivity to my

plea for compassion and care for my well-being. Her inability to show that compassion and care was like a gaping wound. I told her that this was definitely going to happen. Dad said he loved me and was sure things would turn out fine. Done.

Next, and hardest, was telling my girls. Needless to say, they had already been turned inside out when Bill and I had begun living separately a year earlier. Even though marital separation is the sort of thing kids can get at some level—separations and divorces do occur with regularity—I was aware it had substantially rattled them. This next crisis, however—an eating disorder so mammoth it required me to leave them for a month—was much harder to understand. When I left for a month for the vision quest and Cabin trip, the girls had been at sleepaway camp, and presumably my absence affected them little. Furthermore, they had shown no recognition of my eating problems, as kids often normalize their situations. Years later, however, they recognized the extreme nature of my behavior, including my dieting. They acknowledged, too, how they mimicked my unhealthy behavior by resorting to unnecessary diets in their preteen years.

I assembled them for a talk, and they huddled up with the family dog, shifting uneasily. We were in the den, usually our place for family games or TV viewing. I took a breath and began explaining how I had been using food as a crutch to cope with my problems, trying to make food into something it couldn't provide. As a result, I had developed a serious, full-fledged eating disorder. I was in trouble and had to get professional help, and I was going away for a month to get treatment and get well.

Nothing I said elicited a visible reaction from them. I said I would miss them terribly and would come home a more together person and better mom. I added what I hoped was the comforting news that their dad would be returning to be with them in our home while I was gone. That caused them to look up, finally, at each other and at me, and both managed small smiles. They asked a few questions, petting the dog and looking down or away during my answers. We ended with a hug and off they went, with a casual, "Good luck, Mom. We understand. Love you." Done.

Off I went to the Woodbridge Clinic's Eating Disorder Unit. I acclimated better than I had imagined I would, making significant progress the first two weeks and looking forward to my release in two more. Then, the therapists and counselor treating me delivered a zinger: in their view, I needed a longer-term program.

My counselor reminded me that as part of the treatment, we revealed our life story, and they, in turn, looked to uncover places where our disease hid. This allowed them to fashion the treatment to uproot the disease like a pernicious weed. She said that eating disorders, in particular, often confounded with misdirection. Consider exercise, for example. Who would ever think a disciplined exercise enthusiast who never missed a day of exercise, regardless of weather or other schedule considerations, could in doing so be servicing not a healthy lifestyle but an unhealthy or even desperate addiction? In my situation, the therapists had concluded that my eating disorder had disguised itself in my obsessive exercise patterns. After all, wasn't the goal to burn calories, and lots of them? They were on to me. There was a conspiracy among my purging, laxatives, and excessive exercise, all fueled by my inability to control my food intake. I had created a "combo" addiction, a sort of mix and match that kept me "safe" from weight gain and other outer symptoms.

The clinical therapist chimed in, citing how I had handled my second pregnancy with Cecily years before. She reminded me how, as I had recounted to them, my doctors had placed me on bed rest for the duration of my third trimester—but I had found this unacceptable. I fancied myself invincible, different from other patients, and believed that nothing bad could happen to me. Besides, I had a toddler and a job. How could I stay in bed? So I hadn't. Of course, I not only rejected bed rest—I had to keep exercising, too. While going for a run a few days after this medical directive, I broke water early, and Cecily arrived seven weeks premature, appearing with a patent ductus arteriosus, a congenital heart disorder that can be life threatening if not treated immediately. Cecily remained in the hospital ICU for three weeks, where I fed her my pumped breast milk through an eyedropper until she was strong enough to breast-feed.

This pried my eyes open, and I began to see my addiction through a different lens. If more evidence were needed, they reminded me that I began using laxatives at the tender age of twelve, whenever "I felt fat," thus establishing an early foundation for my lifelong ingrained eating disorder. I got the point. With heavy head and heart, I acquiesced to extended treatment.

Woodridge, however, was not a long-term facility. I needed a placement elsewhere. Woodridge recommended Pathways in

Florida. I feared relapse and coveted recovery after coming this far, so I signed up for a month at Pathways, leaving Woodbridge soon after my first two weeks there. I called Bill to get his agreement to stay longer in the house. No problem there. He understood my commitment to putting my life back together. We did not discuss our marriage.

I realized that confronting my problems this way also meant my relationship with Gymboree might be approaching a more formal end. I decided to approach Stuart about my equity position in the company. I had enough presence of mind, with my marriage on the rocks and my health in jeopardy, to want a nest egg to secure my future. Like many entrepreneurs, I dreamt of $1 million as the important number to achieve. I knew that having this money could buy me the time I would need to heal. I did not get sick overnight, and I would not get well overnight.

Gymboree was a private company with no liquidity. So when I asked Stuart to consider acquiring my stock, it would have been fair for him to reply, "What nerve!" He was reluctant at first and suggested I consider further—not because he was unwilling to acquire my interest but because he believed so strongly in Gymboree and its financial future. He wanted to protect me from what could prove to be a shortsighted financial play.

I told him I would ponder it further and thanked him for considering my best interests. He suggested I hold on to as much stock as I could, and he would buy whatever portion I chose to give up for an equitable price. Then, he made a magnanimous gesture that spoke volumes about Stuart Moldaw. He added that if the company went public within eighteen months of any deal we made, he would rip the deal up and return my stock as if that deal had never happened. This, he explained, would protect me from the loss of a significant financial return if something happened within a reasonable time of the transaction. The offer stunned me. Despite my battle wounds, I understood how fully Stuart believed in Gymboree. I decided to take some time to consider whether to sell and if so to what extent, which relieved him.

Not long after, I arrived at Miami International Airport and headed to Pathways. Almost a half-hour into the trip, the taxi exited the freeway to drive on local surface streets. Within a couple of minutes, the taxi stopped in front of a nondescript office building with no signage in the middle of a mixed residential and commercial neighborhood. I looked around to locate the attractive property where Pathways presumably sat, but there was nothing in view but dull apartment buildings. Was my driver lost? Then, the driver shifted the gears into park and flipped on the hazard blinkers, which moved me to ask, "Why are we stopping here?" He matter-of-factly responded, "Lady, this is where you told me to go." I didn't realize it at the time, but I was about to enter my own Twilight Zone.

After checking in, I was shown to my quarters in an apartment building a few blocks away. Each accommodation housed four residents in a two-bedroom suite. In other words, I would live with these other people and share a bedroom, a far cry from my hip turn-of-the-century home in idyllic Mill Valley. My judgments were running faster than my beloved Cabin's American River after snowmelt.

Before too long, I met two of my three roommates. The first, Geneen, was in her twenties and suffered from anorexia. She had recently been released from a hospital after being held for a month—a stay that extended so long, she told me, because she had refused to eat, and when she had been forcibly hooked up with intravenous feeding tubes she had kept removing them, out of fear she would "get fat" or be poisoned by "whatever it was" they were putting inside her. This horrified me. She had been 85 pounds when she entered the hospital and was now only about 95 pounds.

My other roommate, Jan, was closer to 250 pounds, and was, like me, in her forties. She had a daughter Meegan's age and a son in his early twenties. Jan was a social worker, a respected professional and a good mom who appeared functional, despite having participated in several different treatment programs over the years. When I showed a look of alarm at her treatment history, she noted: "Very tricky disease from which to recover," a virtual mantra I would hear over and over at Pathways. Each time I heard it, I held my breath. Jan had been at Pathways for two months and was my assigned "big sister," if you will. I liked her; she was a sweetheart, even though her obesity put me off initially. I wondered if our third roommate, expected to arrive in a few days, would be more like me or "them."

As soon as I had time to myself after meeting more of the women residents, I started to bargain with myself again. The monologue went something like this: *These women have serious problems and I do not. I'm nothing like them—most are college age, have had little outside success, and—unlike me—are veterans of Wood-bridge-type treatment facilities. Am I that sick? I am quite functional and just need a little help with food stuff and exercise. This whole thing is a huge mistake. Maybe I bolt before I unpack?* I thought I had been in over my head at Gymboree, but I was really unprepared for this.

My thoughts eventually returned to that vulnerable and help-less woman in the first-aid tent. I remembered how surrendered I had felt then, and again when the Woodbridge professionals helped me confront the self-defeating patterns connected to my wily disease. I thought about Jan, and part of me recognized that had I taken responsibility for the amount of food I ingested, I might not look much different. Facing that reality was painful. Jan was my reflection in many ways. I softened inside—which was not easy for me after years of living in my carefully con-structed walled city. I wanted to trust that I was in the right place. Maybe I *was* that sick. I cautiously took the leap of faith.

The work began at Pathways. We always worked in groups, with no individual therapy. Our sessions took place in the of-fice building where I had reported on arrival, which also housed commercial finance companies, mortgage brokers, and the like. This format, focused on finding common ground among group members and stressing that everyone mattered, mirrored the collaborative style I used at Gymboree. That was a good fit for me, and the group-therapy mind-set allowed me to suspend ego in favor of honoring others and the group.

As we exposed ourselves in the safety of the Pathways offices, we realized we were not alone. I began to see how our problems had all evolved from the same emotional cloth. My heart softened and my edges smoothed. Regular exposure to people battling similar demons began to strengthen and heal me. Viewing each of us as mirrors of one another dismantled the delusion that our disease was unique to each of us. Over time, I lost my bravado; our community had real curative powers. The more honesty I produced about myself, the stronger I felt and the more committed to stay the course.

The emphasis on the power of the community kept bringing me back to Gymboree, especially its earlier days, when I would urge my colleagues to see legacy as our collective work, to find power and purpose in a unified mission and not individual agendas. The more we suspended superficiality and personal issues, and embraced our roles to serve the group, the more meaningful our individual performances, and the more successful our work as a whole.

As our Pathways community dug deep together, our physical differences melted away. The disease was the same for each of us, only with different manifestations. We each wanted to cut the chains of our imprisonment, to be set free and gain acceptance for ourselves. Rejection terrified us, ensnaring us in the hell we knew versus the fear of what we did not know. In just a few weeks, I already felt the potency of this collective healing, with the able assistance of our lead therapists, Margaret and Deirdre. Contemporaries of mine, and both loving and no-nonsense types, Margaret and Deirdre had themselves walked the arduous road of recovery from food addiction. That they had made it to the other side comforted me.

Mindful that our success turned on entrusting them with our welfare, I was reminded of that turning point at Gymboree when, unable to summon the energy and creativity needed to overcome the Hasbro debacle, I turned to my staff to divine a business solution. I had not stood on ceremony or asserted my CEO prerogative. At Pathways, I felt safe doing what they told me to do. Crazy. I was more compliant than I had ever been as a child, or when I'd had differences with our board of directors.

As I was about to learn, the particulars of my treatment plan, beyond the group therapy, depended on a foundation-altering sequence of life changes—deprivations, one might say, designed to confront my disease at its heart. First up, of course, was food itself. Here, we ate for subsistence only. There was no more, "Hmm, what do I feel like eating?" That privilege was lost to us, certainly for now, maybe indefinitely. I had to learn that food was, at bottom, sustenance and not a tool for assuaging emotions.

We each, accordingly, got a food plan. Mine was a weight-maintenance plan; my present weight, apparently, was appropriate for me. What a concept! I had almost no trust that my body could maintain a consistent weight, since to me it had always been in flux, like a department store elevator, going up or down on the whim of the passengers who entered. I thought it would take a miracle to maintain a consistent weight, given my erratic history. Margaret assured me it would happen. None of us, she said, knew our true weight. People in the throes of this craziness weighed themselves dozens of times a day, assessing values by the half-pound. We learned that our real value had nothing to do with a number on a scale.

The food plan identified the amount of protein, carbohydrates, and so on we could eat each day. We planned our meals each night, wrote them down, posted them on the refrigerator, and pledged to our sponsor to stay true to what we posted. That was it. All food was weighed and measured. Once a week we were weighed, standing on the scale backward, a practice that, decades later, I still observe.

Our weekly $40 food allowance was earmarked solely for groceries. We prepared all our meals in our meager apartments, three times a day, with a yogurt snack before bed unless on a weight-loss plan. Week after week I sustained my weight, neither gaining nor losing. I loved that after all the abuse my body had suffered at my hands, it could return to normalcy and health with relative ease. To my relief, the world began to seem more manageable. I was beginning to feel grounded.

I spent my first Thanksgiving away from family. Slicing turkey and weighing my quarter-pound allotment on a scale was humbling, to say the least. I knew that if I could embrace this perspective, I would see it as a gift. To surrender, to be unmasked, was to be liberated. Later, I learned these words of Ai Weiwei, the extraordinary Chinese artist: "Maybe to be powerful is to be fragile." Often it is the most troubled times that endow us with our most penetrating insights and confer the most lasting sense of gratitude.

Margaret next removed all exercise from my daily routine in order to ease the endorphin rushes that kept flushing through my system. I was not even permitted to walk up the stairs to my fourth-floor apartment, which eliminated the possibility I might use the stair climb as an aerobic activity. I had to take the elevator. She had me figured out. I was forced to sit on the sidelines during the biweekly exercise class. I was disconsolate at first, but I hung on.

Each of these rules, whether in isolation or collectively, might strike many as harsh, unnecessary, or autocratic. Yet, as the woman who lived them, I felt the curative power of giving up something that before had felt so integral to my life. As I accepted the new conditions of my recovery, I became stronger and more mature. My new world order featured a beautiful blend of surrender and trust that helped forge my transformation and deepen my commitment to recovery.

My treatment plan also called for "feelings-only" days. I spoke only when I could say, "I feel . . ." and add a "feeling adjective." To help me identify the subtle range of human emotions and what I might be feeling, Margaret gave me a copious list of terms for expressing human sentiment. It was of no consequence if I spewed non sequiturs when what I was feeling had little or nothing to do with what was going on around me, or even if what I said might be hurtful to others. I was to be raw and spontaneous. The emphasis on the expression of feelings was so fundamental to my treatment that I was exempted on our "gentle meal" days from the general charge that we eat in silence. The gentle meal day was designed to let us experience how communication can occur through eye contact and other subtler expressions and gestures.

The Pathway professionals also had more invasive tactics in store for me. They knew the comfort I garnered from my casual yet deliberate style of dress, which prompted them to forbid me from wearing the clothes I had brought, as a way to sever attachments to my prior way of life. They also confiscated my makeup. I was supplied each morning with a pair of no-nonsense jeans and a plain T-shirt to wear, while the clothes I had brought were kept in a drawer.

One of the least conventional aspects of my treatment had to do with the stuffed animal I was required to carry with me everywhere, inside the program and out in public, as a way to put me in touch with the vulnerable little girl inside. The stuffed animal requirement flashed me back to my days as a little girl and "my" doll collection. On trips to Europe, my mother would buy beautiful, rosy-cheeked dolls that were kept pristine inside a mammoth locked curio cabinet that hung on the wall across from my small bed. When I was very young, I would often bury my head in a pillow to evade their frozen gazes. When I was good, she would unlock the curio cabinet so I could choose a single doll to hold—but no cuddling, undressing, or fiddling with the doll's hair were allowed. I longed to receive the same adoring look I saw in Mom's eyes when we took out those dolls.

Bandit, my stuffed raccoon, was no doll. She came with me to Publix, the grocery market; to and from my apartment and the office building of Pathways; and to the public twelve-step meetings we attended in the evenings. After a while, I lost my self-consciousness, no longer concerned what people thought as I moseyed about with my furry little companion. Bandit served as a constant reminder of the vulnerable parts of myself I had failed to protect.

My one-month stay at Pathways proved too short. The professional staff was unequivocal in its opinion that I needed a long-term stay to gain trustworthy recovery. They were non-committal on how long but recommended at least a few more months. My first reaction was to think about how this would affect my daughters and my relationship with them. Pathways compounded the distress of separation by limiting me to a single phone call a week with my daughters, and none with Bill and my folks. But once the dust settled on this difficult condition, I embraced that edict as therapeutic and not punishing. I missed Meegan and Cecily deeply. I also knew, however, that my ability to parent them, model for them, and form indelible bonds with them as they moved into adulthood depended on my regaining my life. Rather than rail against what seemed unfair, almost regressive, I trusted the treatment and knew that focusing un-waveringly on recovery and on the present rather than the past would deliver the tomorrow for which I longed. My ability to take the long view for my girls and me, while suffering pangs of separation during the expansive interim, was an important step in my recovery.

I knew, in my heart, that my marriage to Bill was on bor-rowed time and, while legally alive, would wind down and die in the not-too-distant future. My company was in good hands and, regardless, my Gymboree days were rapidly coming to a close. I had brought the company to a great place—I knew that much. The brand was strong and new leadership was poised to gain even greater success. The irony is that the success I led the company to had rendered me fungible and obsolete. Nonetheless, I did not long for Gymboree at this point. I longed for my recovery. I was voting for myself.

I was reminded of the cynical comment I had made to Margaret during my first week, about being brainwashed, to which Margaret had retorted, to gales of laughter, "Your brain needs washing!" This proved no overstatement. She deftly and humorously exposed my mixed-up thinking. Raw and ready, I began to see myself well enough to advance the building process. This time the business was me, and the mission was to get healthy, get strong.

CHAPTER 16

⚬⚬⚬⚬⚬⚬⚬⚬⚬⚬⚬⚬⚬⚬⚬⚬⚬⚬⚬⚬⚬⚬⚬⚬⚬⚬⚬⚬⚬⚬

Quintessential Entrepreneurism

I WAS BUILDING an internal strength that fueled a steady climb toward recovery when, after four months at Pathways, Margaret recommended that I stay even longer. She underscored how I was advancing, and how more time would deepen my recovery's roots and give me more time to practice new habits in a controlled and less chaotic world. I felt the progress. I could sense the value of more time and foresee the inevitability of full recovery—which was my priority, above all. And, so, feeling grounded in the program and its routines, I accepted without protest. I informed Bill about the longer stay, and he accepted without much comment. I spoke to the girls, and while the conversation was difficult and stilted, they seemed to understand, especially since

I told them I was making steady progress and that, with the approval of Pathways, I would visit them for Cecily's sweet sixteen celebration.

The first few months flew by, and, as hoped, Pathways gave me the green light to return home for Cecily's sixteenth birthday celebration in April of 1991. Wonderful as it was to see my girls, the familiar home surroundings made me feel uneasy, and I knew I needed more time at Pathways before I could safely return. Little by little, I began to trust myself. I could listen to my inner voices, discern their perspectives, and align their concerns—much as I had tried to do with the people I led as CEO. Seeing the kinship to my business leadership style was comforting. I knew and trusted my sense of inner knowing about the best course, compromising and bringing consensus to all the voices within me that clamored for attention. Like never before, my internal voices called for stability and measured living. Each passing week, my resolve for recovery strengthened and my comfort with myself settled deeply into my core. This time the ability to act was for my best interest. My core axis shifted, and I sought a "steady as she goes" confidence to claim with humble gratitude this new internal CEO position. I knew, too, how unwavering my commitment had to be in each decision I made for myself. This kind of consistency propelled me in a positive direction, where my decisions reflected what I felt was best for me, not what others expected of me.

Our counselors staged a gift exchange event that became pivotal in my recovery. Here's how it worked: you picked something meaningful of yours to give away to someone else—on a permanent basis, not a loan. The selection had to hold singular importance, the item had to be difficult to part with, and—critically—you had to know it was time for you to let it go. The more attached you were to it, the more healing derived, so it was said. You wrapped the gift in aluminum foil and placed it on a pile with the others in the center of a circle.

Next, one by one, we each chose a package. Like a well-ordered Christmas morning, each package was unwrapped separately, with the recipient finding out then both the giver and the story of why the giver chose that particular gift. Becky opened my gift, and as she did, the room gasped. It was my wedding ring, which had not left my hand for more than 22 years prior to its ceremonial aluminum foil–wrapping that morning. I was facing the truth about my marriage; like my marriage to Gymboree, it was over, and parting with the ring symbolized the end. My well-being depended upon having courage about my future. Meanwhile, Becky had always hoped to marry, and never had. Perhaps my ring portended good things for her.

When we completed the gift exchange, I felt a calm like the one I'd felt when we opted to pursue the retail strategy after Hasbro. In both instances, I could not know the outcome, yet I knew what I had to do. That night, without hesitation, I called Bill and encouraged him to come to Miami for mediation. The time had come to end our marriage.

This fueled another major decision: how to handle the stock deal with Stuart Moldaw. I was ready to act on that decision as well. I called Stuart, to whom I had given only sketchy details about my decision to extend my stay at Pathways. As promised, he had my back; he had made sure Gymboree continued to pay my salary during my stay. I would never have considered asking for that, yet, when it happened, I felt respected and honored. When we spoke, after minimal pleasantries and updates, I got right to it.

"Stu, I have been thinking for some time about your generous willingness to purchase my stock. It has been months since we spoke about this, and I appreciate your patience."

"Yes, Joan, I remember, and everything I offered then still stands, including that you may rescind the whole deal if the company goes public within the next eighteen months." He was, as he had always been, clear and to the point with me.

"Stuart, I am prepared to take you up on the deal. It will give me some comfort as I move into whatever is next for me. Thank you—I have learned so much about business, character, and life from you."

He thanked me, too, and told me again how special I was and how great Gymboree was. He stressed that my legacy would forever be embedded in the company's culture. I couldn't absorb all of that, although I did hear him say he would have papers prepared, including something for Bill to sign, as California was a community-property state. We agreed that I would retain 30 percent of my current holdings and then sell the remaining 70 percent to him in exchange for $1 million. As promised, the agreement provided for rescission of the entire deal if Gymboree went public within eighteen months—a uniquely magnanimous gesture, and even more so considering the passage of time since he had made the original offer. Before we said goodbye, he let me know that the company continued apace, albeit with some speed bumps, and told me not to worry—he was bringing in the "right talent." While the news pleased me, I felt detached. And, while it was so Stuart for him to end the call with business, I saw it as his giving me due respect as founder, CEO, and chairman emeritus.

I returned to my current job, the work of rebuilding myself. I was starting to see how the tightly focused Pathways treatment methodology both dug out damaged roots and planted new seedlings. Practicing new life skills was like learning a new sport; they took time to become second nature. Little by little, I felt the seedlings growing roots. Transparency and vulnerability were not significant values expressed in my family. On the contrary, I had been taught to keep private anything that could damage the family's standing; "it is nobody's business" was the party line. "Put on a happy face" was no mere cute expression or song lyric, but code for "keep your discomfort to yourself," which was the expectation at home and the rule in the outside world. Gradually, about a month or so after returning from California for Cecily's birthday bash, I felt empowered and ready to face life outside the comforts of the Pathways community.

Not long after the gift exchange, after a total of eight months in treatment, Pathways announced it was time to take a major step toward completing my treatment. I was ready to undergo preparation to reenter "the world." This entailed getting a job, venturing out each day to work, returning for dinner, and sharing my experiences in the evening groups. It was the final phase of the treatment plan, a transitional tool to facilitate a return to our separate lives, experience life on its terms, and test our new coping skills. Could I maintain emotional stability with the inevitable life triggers?

I was pumped. My heart raced as I scanned the *Miami Herald* want ads, in an excited search for a suitable placement. Instantaneously, I envisioned myself dressed the part and off to work in a marketing position, maybe managing a franchise or start-up, or doing consulting—you name it. Even anticipating the upcoming interviews felt like a high. Bring it on!

As my reverie peaked, Margaret summoned me to her office for a private meeting. One-on-ones with her were rare, which meant something major was up. In the heart-to-heart that followed, she told me that unlike the other women headed to traditional workplaces, Pathways had designed something different for me, a placement tailored specifically to my treatment goals. My breath tightened and I froze up; whatever was coming, I couldn't imagine it was good.

"Joan, we have zero concerns about your capability and talent in the job marketplace. The team sees the placement we have in mind as a valuable opportunity to expand your considerable capabilities on other levels. We believe strongly in your ability to broaden."

The puzzlement on my face had to be as conspicuous as it felt. I managed to say, "I'm not sure I follow, Margaret."

"Let me explain, Joan. We have found a placement for you as a volunteer. Please understand, while this is not a paying job, it has the requisite responsibilities. And it has two major treatment benefits: it avoids the kind of competitive environment that could retrigger your demons, and it gives you more time to develop your growing sense of wellness and satisfaction from acts of kindness that get no acknowledgment, absent the pressure of external measures."

"Still not getting it," is all I could get out.

"You will be volunteering at the Alzheimer's day care facility at the Jewish Home for the Aged," she announced. "This volunteer work is the final phase of your treatment at Pathways."

My instinct was to recoil. I wanted to work, to earn money, to be "valuable." I understood the concern about my limitation to extract personal value from everyday events in the "real" world, and how this volunteer position was an opportunity to grow. No matter. I did not feel up for this challenge. I was afraid I would fail. The irony did not escape me. I had a history of being pretty undaunted in the traditional workplace. But at an Alzheimer's facility, where I'd essentially be invisible and could *not* fail, in traditional terms, I would feel vulnerable. More damning, the thrill of preparing for work, deciding what to wear, getting dressed, all of it, was now irrelevant. No one I worked with there would care about or remember what I looked like. I understood what was expected of me but felt unfit and inadequate. I did not want this placement.

My resistant reaction mocked the handmade "Resiliency" sign hanging above my bed, which I had made my first week at

Pathways to remind myself of my best quality. All of a sudden, the word rang hollow. I felt confident in my recovery from my addictions to food and exercise. That was, after all, why I had come to this place. "Margaret, would you consider letting me just have a simple job?" I asked. My reversion to bargaining revealed that I would try most anything to avoid facing my terror. Her response was simple and disarming: "We at Pathways are confident about the value of this placement for you. Stay with it and be watchful; we are optimistic you will find considerable value in the volunteer work. Please trust us here, Joan." Her conviction in the face of my resistance helped me see how intransigent I could still be—a troublesome holdover from my past.

Of course, I relented. I accepted the placement and became a volunteer at the Jewish Home's Alzheimer's Day Care Center. The clients did not remember me from day to day, even moment to moment. Moreover, I was ancillary, with no real responsibilities, since the paid staff—while thankful for an extra hand—managed fine without a volunteer. Pathways still required me to report on time every day at 9:00 a.m. and stay until 4:00 p.m., when patients were picked up to go home. I was to treat the situation with the respect due a paid position. I needed to derive satisfaction from within myself, through the knowledge I was contributing to others.

In hindsight, this was brilliant treatment. It challenged me to line up internally with what I understood intellectually. It was harder than any near-death challenge I had faced running Gymboree, where I usually succumbed to the loudest and most stubborn of my internal voices. Pathways forced me to mediate these internal battles with greater facility and self-awareness. I knew that only the softer among my internal voices saw sustainable value in the placement. I also knew that I had to quell the louder voices screaming for dominance.

Little by little and day by day, I had recurring moments where I lost myself in the experience and derived pleasure from helping patients eat or move around with ease from one spot to another. Sometimes, we even exchanged warm glances and smiles. Those inspiring moments did not occur every day, yet I cherished them when they did. I more easily embraced this "selfless" service to others knowing that every once in a while there would be a connection like this. Those powerful bits of grace made me forever grateful for the experience. Working in the facility for a few months, processing my feelings, and listening to my treatment companions regale each other about their days expanded my perspective. I began to see my situation as profoundly rewarding, and I shed the initial envy I had of their situations. This turnaround was more daunting than any business challenge I had faced, more invigorating and fulfilling. To this day, I remain in awe of the recovery gifts I experienced through Pathways.

I left Pathways in late summer of 1991, some ten months after leaving California. While steady, I felt protective of my recovery. I was concerned that I needed to move in baby steps before returning to California. I still associated California with the stress of my earlier life, and I was mindful that stress had triggered and escalated my crash. I needed practice dealing with pressure and stress in a healthy way. I wanted humility to replace my former entrepreneurial hubris. I wanted to minimize the risk that I could backslide. It was clear to me that I was not returning to life in California until I felt 100 percent ready. And that was nonnegotiable. I was confident I would get there; I only needed more time to steady myself in my still-new recovery.

Thus, leaving Pathways was not the end of the long recovery road. I had more work to do before returning to my home base. And so I rented a small apartment in Miami near Pathways so I could continue my routines without the daily support of the community. The familiar landscape was comforting. My confidence began to grow. I was up for the next step.

By this time, Bill and I were effectively done. We had participated in mediation in Miami in order to seek a property settlement. And while that effort had not produced a resolution, it was only a matter of time before we allocated our property and had a divorce decree. So, when I met a man named Antonio who captivated me, I was game for a relationship to bring some sense of normalcy to my life outside of Pathways. The relationship was mutually invigorating and respectful; in hindsight, it was also an important part of my recovery path.

I managed a relatively normal life in Miami for about one year. I saw the girls every six weeks, either on visits they made to Miami or during brief trips I made to California. They met Antonio, and while I am sure it was uncomfortable, on the surface the girls and he got along all right, and the four of us meshed well enough. When Antonio was accepted into a post-fellowship program at Yale in 1992, I decided to join him and moved to New Haven. I felt reborn. Meegan and Cecily visited us twice in New Haven and we them twice in California. We talked often on the phone, and I increasingly felt the pull back to the nest, as it were. While I was not quite ready to return, I could see the light at the end of the tunnel. I also felt a need to be productive—not on any grand scale mind you, but a desire to feel more whole than I was feeling. I wanted to do something that contributed to the community, another step in the recovery process.

As my urge to build something welled up, I conceived a new venture that reflected my personal circumstances. Begin from Within, as I called it, initially offered workshops and group meetings for people dealing with eating, weight, and body image issues. I was passionate about everything I had learned during my almost two years of recovery. I partnered with a woman named Marilyn Acquarulo, who I met in the local neighborhood café. Our new venture would be powered by my skill set, her local market understanding, and our shared passion to help people mired in shame. The service work I'd performed at the Alzheimer's center laid the foundation that allowed me to take this next step. This is what I felt I should be doing: bringing things to life for others in ways that expressed my own deep connection to the endeavor. Quintessential entrepreneurism.

In the spring of 1993, I shed the training wheels for good and made my move back to California. Everything I had both feared and prepared for before leaving California had come to pass: my marriage was over, I was no longer part of Gymboree, and I lacked a physical home for my family, as the girls' base camp was with Bill in the home we once had together. Nonetheless, and perhaps craziest of all, I felt truly at home, within myself, with a sense of balance that was better for being bittersweet. I wondered, with cautious hope, what would come next.

CHAPTER 17

∞∞∞∞∞∞∞∞∞∞∞∞∞∞∞∞∞∞∞∞∞∞∞∞∞

I Need Your Company

BEFORE REPLANTING IN California from New Haven, I made a few more major decisions. I came to realize I was not ready for another long-term relationship. I was resolved to trek the next leg of my journey solo, except for the ubiquitous Bandit, the stuffed-animal raccoon that had been at my side since my Pathways days. And Marilyn and I closed Begin from Within, as she had another business that needed her attention and understood my call to return home.

I settled into my new apartment in Los Gatos, the town where I would learn about the Gymboree IPO while having lunch alone at the California Cafe. As it turned out, the IPO landed outside the eighteen-month period of my stock-for-cash deal with Stuart

Moldaw—less than six months outside. The upshot: I kept the cash and Stuart the stock, for which he earned a tidy sum. For me, the deal carried a personal meaning far greater than the lost uptick in wealth. I was neither sad nor had any regret. In one way, my deal with Stuart resounded with what had motivated me about Gymboree in the first place. It had never been about money. It had always been about building something with a dedicated team that shared a vision to help participating families. I moved on, content in the knowledge that I had weathered relatively well what might have been devastating news about "losing" millions of dollars. This empowered me.

By all measures, I had passed the first tests, returning to the area shorn of my marriage, my company, and my home. My one-bedroom rental reminded me more of the unassuming living quarters at Pathways than the chic bungalow in New Haven. Cecily was stoked because I was close to her at the UC Santa Cruz campus and we could hike and do all the things we loved doing together. I still hoped to return to Mill Valley down the road as each step brought me closer. For now, this was home, and I chose it willingly.

Nothing triggered me at the housing complex, likely because I was surrounded by people in similar life situations—not recovering from eating disorders, maybe, but men and women in various stages of life and relationship turbulence. Some were angry and fought, some partied incessantly, others appeared numbed and depressed. The complex had a pool where some gathered at night to work out issues in bellowing voices that drifted into my bedroom window. Conflict was heavy in the air. While the dramatic scenes saddened me, and I kept my distance, I found odd comfort in being among a group not living the picture-perfect life in Northern California. Despite overtures from many of my neighbors to engage me as a sounding board, I set strong boundaries, another beneficial by-product of my work at Pathways.

The funds from Gymboree allowed me time to find my ballast for what was next. I traveled to Europe for the first time, not once, but twice, a few months each time. Sometimes I toured with a friend, sometimes solo. I biked through the south of France and across Tuscany from Florence to Italy's Elba Island. I went on a safari in Africa and made the climb up Mt. Kilimanjaro, one of world's great "seven summits" and the only one not requiring technical climbing expertise. I became a tourist in Paris and Barcelona, visited the Basque country, and more. Those experiences, plus time, yielded a strong sense that my recovery roots were deepening.

I bought a modest home in Los Gatos. Meegan and Cecily came often for sleepovers, and I entertained others more comfortably than I could in my little apartment. My life was widening, and I began doing some consulting. I connected with an old Gymboree colleague, Marcia Jaffe, and collaborated on some significant marketing projects. Happily, I was still well regarded in the kids industry and clients came effortlessly. I was grateful that my chops appeared intact. We did excellent work. I enjoyed the engagements, yet I felt something missing. I learned that I preferred being at the center of the action. Good to know.

I also sensed something stirring from my travels; I felt urges to go home and reclaim my history. I needed to complete the circle. Was I ready? I wasn't sure.

Before I was able to figure this out, Meegan, Cecily, and I traveled to Thailand over the holidays in 1994–1995 and biked through the Golden Triangle. Mountain biking for two weeks in the backcountry with my daughters was a once-in-a-lifetime trip, as we traversed primitive villages outside of Chiang Mai and Chiang Rai. We also went to Myanmar, aka Burma. At the border, uniformed men confiscated our passports and, when I protested, pushed us into the chaos and confusion on the other side of the double chain-link fences. It was frightening. We wandered the markets among daunting crowds, curious faces staring at our intrusion into their world, then elbowed our way back through the throngs of shoving and staring people and convinced the un-fazed men to return our passports. Something shifted inside me. I realized I was ready to go home—to my real home, our family town, Mill Valley. I guess everything seemed doable compared with being trapped in a country against your will.

On my return from Thailand, Karen Robbins, still a dear friend from our JCC job-share days, dragged me to my first yoga class, despite my objecting, "I do not think that is for me." While no longer an exercise addict, I couldn't connect the exhilaration of my recent Mt. Kilimanjaro ascent to sitting on a mat with my legs crossed and making guttural sounds. Another recovery tru-ism—*progress not perfection*—applied, as I watched my judgmen-tal thoughts choke possibility. I was still prone to be shortsighted and self-limiting. Sweet Karen held her ground: "Give it a try. I need your company." Friendship trumped my reservations, and I went with her.

What happened next cracked my heart open. My yoga experience transformed me as no exercise ever had. The release and rejuvenation enveloped me. Every cell of my being flushed with renewed balance and life force. If you asked me what happened in that first class, I could not explain it in any rational way. Holding back the urge to sob, I allowed a few soft tears to flow as we practiced the ancient sun salutations in a facility aptly named YogaStudio.

As I later came to understand yoga practice better, I learned that each physical pose, or asana—together with focused breathing, and particularly when sequenced well—engenders a natural, healing connection among body, mind, and spirit. We experience a kind of internal cleansing, a bath of fresh oxygenated blood to our organs and brain. The attendant afterglow is revitalizing, generating feelings of well-being and release. I appreciated yoga's way of fostering self-reconnection and equanimity. As I took up the practice and became a regular student, I found that the connection among the community of other students crystallized the experience. It was unimportant if I knew you by name; it was enough to feel your presence on a mat next to, behind, or in front of me. We each had our own personal experience while mindful of the power surge of the collected yogis around us, and how our sangha (the group) escalated the experience for all.

As I became a devotee and learned more and more, I found

myself less and less interested in the driving physical activities I used to pursue. I lost the appetite for adrenaline-rush activities. Soon, mountain hikes and yoga were my dual passions. Yoga became the cornerstone of my sustained recovery.

I was also back in builder mode. I longed to make real the Begin from Within pilot I'd launched in New Haven almost three years earlier. I wanted to offer ongoing groups and workshops to help end the isolation of people suffering from eating disorders. I envisioned that these groups could help women address food, weight, and body issues. Term it giving back, or maybe zealousness, but I felt the call.

And so I relaunched Begin from Within. My thought was to hire seasoned therapists who understood the complexity of eating disorders and shared my philosophy (based on my personal experience) of working in groups, as opposed to the one-on-one methodology. Recent research by Helen Riess, MD, and J. Scott Rutan, PhD, of the Harvard Medical School had shown that the favored treatment for eating disorders was open-ended psychodynamic group therapy, and those who participated in such groups with others struggling with similar behaviors had far more promising and lasting recoveries than those who pursued one-on-one therapy of any modality, despite the claims of traditional clinicians.

The threshold question I faced was whether to create a for-profit or nonprofit business. Begin from Within mirrored aspects of early Gymboree: it was a service for like-minded people; a program where time spent together had a positive impact on emotional well-being; a self-sustaining experience that improved with repetition and, with good results, required no marketing; a place where the leader played a key role in creating the group dynamic. There was, however, a significant difference between the two concepts.

Gymboree blossomed in a pre–social media era where its popularity spread through broad word of mouth and guerilla marketing in all forms. Attendees, moms in particular, were virtual billboards for the program, excited to encourage others to sign up for Gymboree. The participants in Begin from Within, on the other hand, carried personal shame that inhibited enrollment, much less the inclination to proselytize the program's benefits. People suffering from these addictions, regardless of degree, faced public opprobrium.

For that reason, from the get-go, Begin from Within looked like an uphill battle as a commercial business. Developing a marketing plan workable enough to sustain profitability was a severe challenge. I reasoned that growing Begin from Within as a nonprofit would help us attract media attention, giving us visibility and credibility with our client market. We would avoid any profit-motive questions that might dampen our aspirations to do good work. My mission was to help and help only.

I decided to proceed on a nonprofit basis. I was willing to fund Begin from Within with my own money to get it off the ground, so I created a donor-advised fund with the well-respected nonprofit Jewish Family and Children's Services in San Francisco, where I had joined the board. I hoped others would contribute to the fund if my initial grant was insufficient to get us to break even.

It worked! Begin from Within attracted and helped a wide variety of people on the continuum of food-related issues. We received wonderful press and, by late 1996, we were operating in several Bay Area counties, including Marin. Around then, a woman named Jackie Dwyer, who owned YogaStudio, saw some of our favorable press coverage and called me, unaware that I was an avid student at her own studio. She offered YogaStudio space for Begin from Within workshops.

Synchronicity is a beautiful thing and I never take any of it for granted. Jackie and I formed a friendship. While the YogaStudio space was not right for Begin from Within, Jackie and I had many discussions about the healing and liberating power of yoga. She thought her business could use some fresh ideas and my experience in business rendered me a good candidate to help her.

By the summer of 1997, Begin from Within was firmly established; I had recruited fifteen therapists and an excellent woman to head up the whole program. Although I checked in regularly, Begin from Within no longer needed my attention. We had received countless heartfelt thank-you letters from participants, and everyone involved felt tremendous gratification. The start-up phase was complete, and just as I had learned at Gymboree, the professionals could take it from there. The timing was ripe for me to devote my time and energy to a new entrepreneurial venture. I had come to honor that I was a natural entrepreneur, a builder. I needed to give full expression to my whole self, but simply—or not so simply—needed to stay vigilant so that my creative energies did not overwhelm the other parts of me. At this point, I had been abstinent for almost seven years, which I thought had a neat congruence with the idea that humans renew all their body cells every seven years. Whether this is scientifically true or not, I liked the coincidence. I felt an honest rebirth, a surge of confidence, an urge to go for it.

Jackie and I became partners at YogaStudio in 1997. I invested $200,000 for a 50 percent share of a business that was grossing not that much more per year when I came on board. After taking a yoga teacher training in order to teach classes myself, I was full on. While we had a vibrant and growing yoga community, profitability required greater scale, which opened the door to a marketing and business development plan. The first business step was finding a larger space. We secured a new location a few blocks away from the original Mill Valley studio on the main street in town. We more than doubled in size, with two practice rooms, full-service showers, and a comfortable lobby for tea and boutique shopping. The new studio was scheduled to open in March 1998. At the original Mill Valley studio, as well as at local vendors and shops, we posted renderings of the upcoming location, architectural layouts, photos, and progress updates.

We initiated a charter membership program for preregistrants, a model that featured unlimited monthly classes. This was a radical departure from the model of purchasing class packs. I wanted to promote a fuller sense of belonging among the students, helping them understand yoga practice as an integral part of their lives. Members were no longer "called to the desk" when they were out of classes to purchase more. This approach built loyalty and was all but revolutionary in this fledgling industry (though it was standard in the fitness field), as the roots of yoga were donation-based. The bold switch to automatic credit card deductions worked, even though our monthly fees were greater than those of most gyms. We were pure yoga, and not a hybrid program of classes held in a gym full of exercise equipment.

Months before opening our full campaign, the early returns were gangbusters. We posted the names of charter members on the wall to highlight their commitment. We offered a $99 monthly fee deal as a one-time offer that was not subject to increase, as long as the charter member kept a current membership. Our goal, by the time of the studio opening, was to secure a few hundred committed members, all on credit card autopay. We made it! We had bucked tradition and in the process increased cash flow, improved financial planning, and created a loyal and committed yogi community. The grand opening of our large new studio was indeed grand. It had free classes, media fuss, and charter members making merry, all fostering the buzz. My hopes for early profitability rose.

A few months later, we hit a bump in the road. Jackie decided to return to her native Los Angeles and wanted me to buy her out. I had little choice. She was going and I was disinclined to have a silent partner. I took the plunge with no ambition greater than to run a small community business that lined up on all fours with the person I was becoming. Sometimes things happen and we must go with the flow. More often than not, we hear how different businesses develop from similar stories. Be prepared to hop on the bus when it stops in front of you! First it was Gymboree, then it was Begin from Within, and now it was YogaStudio.

My new world, however, was about to get complicated. As I found yoga, I also met Steve Strauss. Steve and I were the beneficiaries of the conspiratorial matchmaking of our respective daughters, who were college roommates. We both had come through long-term Mill Valley marriages, and despite all four of our daughters knowing one another and our homes being in close proximity, we had never met. Meeting Steve renewed the possibility of great love in my life. It also meant the opportunity to forge a new home base for our college-student daughters. I was amazed and thankful that two years after coming back home to Mill Valley in 1995, I had been able to find new love, new passion, and a new entrepreneurial challenge.

Not much more than a year had passed after our initial lunch when Steve and I got married. The girls couldn't believe it. At our wedding, they giggled in disbelief. Not so much over the marriage, which they were thrilled about, but more that I would be willing to sing with Steve in front of all our guests. Didn't I know that I couldn't sing? Yes, I knew—and I did it anyway. Steve and I rehearsed 10,000 times, or so it seemed, Joe Cocker's "You Are So Beautiful." Even harmony! Historical fears of embarrassment, judgment, and even shame had largely melted away in my life. Feeling protected, I took many more new risks in addition to singing out loud. It was liberating. Our families soon became a uniquely blended Brady Bunch. All four of our daughters had a stake in our establishing happy new home bases both in Mill Valley and at the Cabin.

And then trouble—serious trouble.

Steve fell ill shortly after we married. I had noticed signs of something amiss almost from the beginning, for example, forgetfulness, habitual lateness, difficulty maintaining his attention, a distorted sense of time. Steve was a remarkably creative soul, a designer, musician, and artist, and I dismissed these little oddities as the left-brain idiosyncrasies of an artist less than focused on life's immediate details. I did not want to imagine anything else. Then, two years after our wedding, while we were on a yoga holiday in Greece, Steve had a major stroke that induced paralysis on one side and distorted his speech. We were in Crete, hours from any hospital—not that doctors could have done much of anything even had we been ten minutes away.

After a few days in a hospital in Knossos, where they spoke little English, we returned to San Francisco and consulted the top neurologist at the University of California San Francisco (UCSF) medical center. The diagnosis: multi-infarct dementia. Steve apparently had already suffered a series of imperceptible small strokes before the big one on Crete, which explained the intermittent small lapses. Worse, the doctor explained that this diagnosis meant Steve would continue to suffer strokes and his condition would worsen, and, regrettably, as it did, he would lose his emotional and mental facilities as well as his physical functions. The process would be gradual and the timing of his diminishment unpredictable. No one could tell which areas of his brain were the most susceptible to these mini-strokes, and thus there was no way to predict which functions would be most affected in the near term versus which would remain intact, at least for several years. One thing was known unequivocally: while the process would be slow, it would be insidious and inevitable.

How do you process such a horrendous forecast moments after your husband walked easily into the office and listened and understood, not to mention after having made love that morning and made plans for dinner and a movie after the appointment? Our life for the moment was OK, wasn't it? As the hip neurologist in Greece had said, in his limited English, in response to my volley of questions, "the brain is a mystery." This was perhaps the most profound insight out of the many medical pronouncements I would receive over the next several years. At first Steve seemed to comprehend it all and was almost matter-of-fact about the diagnosis. Doctors later explained that the damaged part of his brain had the arduous chore of processing the news. I, on the other hand, was frozen in dread about what might happen over the next few years. In response, in the best spirit of what I learned in recovery, I chose to adopt the slogan, "One day at a time." Another cliché I could (and had to) embrace.

CHAPTER 18

∞∞∞∞∞∞∞∞∞∞∞∞∞∞∞∞∞∞∞∞∞

Unsuited for Surrender

IT WAS NOW 1999, and I did my best to integrate Steve's prognosis into our life as I continued to grow the yoga business. When my buyout of Jackie catapulted me solo to the top spot, I conceived a modest plan: make YogaStudio resemble the success of a small Gymboree franchise operation on a strictly *local* basis. I had in mind a single studio where I taught some of the classes along with the teachers Jackie had assembled. With Nancy Evans, my outstanding manager, I would slowly supplement the teacher roster and build an exemplary small business. I was comfortable I could create a company culture that featured a warm, tight-knit family feeling and strike the right balance between home and business that I had striven to create in the earlier Gymboree days.

Grateful for my hard-earned sense of priorities, I trusted myself to be a true partner not only to Steve but also to the hundreds, if not thousands, of our YogaStudio students.

Despite the foreboding I felt about the future, I also felt I could manage everything, however harrowing, so long as I maintained my abstinence. Even when hunkered down in the effort to strengthen the YogaStudio business, my thoughts never drifted far from how badly Steve was declining, or how sad and helpless I felt. Thankfully, my capacity to keep these kinds of things in perspective had grown. I could pretend things were different, but that did not feel very honest. I preferred to cultivate compassion and gentleness to replace any temptation to judge, or to fudge the truth. The deeper my sense of understanding, the more solace I felt. Going to work, far more than just providing balance in my life, was a life-giving respite during this time. Through it, my sense of humanity grew alongside my business savvy. More than anything, focusing on work was how I got through many days. My own yoga practice helped me live in the now as best I could. The ultimate challenge was making sense of the tragic situation with Steve and still finding meaning in my everyday work life. When I could detach enough to become a fly on my own wall, I saw my life with all these different parts of myself in harmony.

A few months passed, and Steve had a second stroke, much more severe and much scarier. I managed to wrestle his dead weight into the car and got him to San Francisco, where he was hospitalized. Several days passed before even minimal movement returned. That portended grave trouble. The longer he was without movement, the more severe the deficit he was likely to suffer.

When Steve was transferred to a rehabilitation center near our home, I went numb, channeling my energies into what I call "admin" mode, to avoid crumbling under my fear of the future. Daily occupational and physical rehabilitation exercises looked unpromising, despite Steve's ongoing efforts. He stayed there for three months, after which all bets were off regarding my earlier sense of harmony. I had lost all the ground I'd gained on how to do this thing. We had entered a new stage of decline.

This latest reality bolt challenged me in a host of ways. What would become of my life? More to the point, how would I show up? How would I be tested? Would I cope? Would my love for Steve prevail? Would my new strength and self-awareness be sustained, and how would they guide me? What kind of relationship would we have? Did I need to plan? Or, was it all about *Be Here Now*, the title of the beautiful, inspiring Ram Dass book that sat dog-eared on my nightstand? Resurrected from my college days, *Be Here Now* had ascended to the first rotation of books that kept me grounded. If I let myself feel everything fully, I was afraid my fear would drown me.

I reverted to a familiar refuse-to-fail perspective: Steve was not going down on my watch. I would use my Gymboree IPO money to get him well. Determined to postpone the inevitable, I focused intently on finding an alternative cure. I was loath to admit that, at best, we could only slow down Steve's irreversible process of diminishment. I couldn't bear losing him. I refused

to accept any likelihood that financial expenditures wouldn't
make a difference. I harbored the fantasy that if I just tried hard
enough, just spent enough, Steve could get fixed, get well, or
even get better. Plus, I knew I wouldn't be able to live with myself
unless I tried everything. I had the stamina for the fight and was
unsuited for surrender, however prudent that course may have
seemed to others.

I was, however, mostly alone in keeping the faith in this
mission. Every professional we consulted cautioned that my attempts to improve Steve's health would be pointless. His daughters and mine stood by observing the continuous efforts and,
while they voiced no objections or opinions, I imagined they
wondered whether I could pull off this miracle. Even if they had
joined the chorus of naysayers about my efforts or my expenditures, I would have heard none of it. I couldn't, and wouldn't. I
was unable to even approach the threshold of letting go. While
different, obviously, in many ways, managing the monumental
challenge to improve Steve's life was no less exacting than running YogaStudio. As I researched stroke and brain injury, I felt
an exploratory buzz akin to what transpires when in an exciting
business start-up mode. I studied a lot and began to feel like a
quasi-expert, especially as I learned that there was so little consensus on treatment and prognosis. It was all up for grabs—I was
up for anything but confirmation that all roads led downhill.

I visited a friend named Phillip Moffitt, an author, Buddhist,
and spiritual teacher, the former editor-in-chief and chief executive of *Esquire* magazine, and the founder of the Life Balance

Institute. Phillip had sage advice that has stayed with me ever since: "Joan, you will have the rare opportunity to line up to your own value system. One day you will know what to do. When you do, it will not matter what anybody thinks—not his children, not yours, not his or your family, and not the community. The right thing to do for you and for Steve will become clear. That day will come, I guarantee." Phillip's counsel became my compass.

The effects of Steve's second stroke did not become truly real until he returned home from rehab. He could barely move, even with a walker, and needed a wheelchair to cover any extended distance. I packed it all in the Toyota and flinched, wondering when or if he would drive again. The pauses between his words made his speech almost painful to listen to. Within a day, I realized that despite his one-word affirmative responses, he lacked the ability to shower, dress, or make even the simplest meal for himself. Every daily task required assistance.

I felt unprepared, alone, and afraid. I bore down and imagined that this was temporary; I couldn't think too far ahead. I hired day-care helpers to spell me when I was at YogaStudio. Coming home after work, I would pretend he was fine. He looked handsome propped up in his favorite oversized oak chair, hardback book in his lap, with Miles Davis playing in the background. Never mind that I had put that music on six hours ago and the book was a prop.

Despite all the therapies, Steve's cognitive capabilities grew more compromised. His diminishment was unsubtly palpable. His executive function, the part of the brain that plans, organizes, and remembers what has happened or needs to be done, was severely impaired. For example, Steve might feel hungry, but be unable to realize what could be done for his hunger or, worse, to know if he had eaten. He was not flippant or disrespectful when he said he did not know if he was hungry or how long ago he had last eaten. He had just lost that brain function. This was tough to make sense of, really tough, and perhaps especially so because no one from the rehab facility had prepared me for the extent of the deficit when they discharged him. He came home with minimal explanation of or advice about his impairments. The social worker taught me the basics of how to use the wheelchair and how to help him in and out of bed and chairs with his limited physical functions. She also gave me pamphlets about cognitive impairments in stroke survivors. The doctor had warned me that I would need care in the home as his condition worsened.

Perplexed and scared, I reverted to my old and not yet fully extinguished pattern, erecting a stoic exterior, although nothing so ominous it would compromise my recovery. Still true to my abstinence in every way, I opted to start seeing a therapist, Roger. I knew I needed sound professional insight and support to navigate this storm. My first challenge, I was told, was to dissolve my proclivity to mimic Mother Teresa, and my second was to sort out the complexity of my various feelings and determine what was best for Steve and me. Neither task would be easy. Roger and I had a strong, affable connection. Our work together could be difficult. The therapeutic lens provided a variant take on Phillip's mystical perspective regarding how to line up with the person I was and where I stood.

As Steve lost more function, my heart broke a little more. My own experience in recovery provided a strong reference point as I struggled to cope. Roger became another pillar. He understood my need to try anything, regardless of how unproductive or futile. He helped me make sense out of my motives rather than talk logic about productive outcomes. He treated my heart with compassion as I mourned, and gradually I traded my cheerleader outfit for a nurse uniform. Soon, he told me, I would find my way to embrace and accept myself rather than try to become someone I was not. The interplay of the steady and wise counsel of Roger and the inspirational words of Phillip enriched and emboldened me.

I had, as the rehab doctors counseled, hired a number of day-care helpers for a few hours here and there so I could comfortably leave Steve alone. About six months later, I hired a man named Rob Horsley, who became Steve's long-term caretaker, and he moved into an in-law unit in our home. Rob and I alternately trotted Steve off to different traditional and alternative therapies: physical, craniosacral, acupuncture, art, hyperbaric oxygen. We added others like Andean shamanism, trial medicines, yoga, and tai chi. We visited dementia and Alzheimer's clinics. I assembled talented musician friends to play for Steve, often using his own vintage guitars and baby grand piano. Most of all, I did my best to shower Steve with unabated love. Rob was a guitarist and adored playing for Steve, which included entertaining him with music Steve himself had written years prior as the well-respected musical impresario of the Blue Bear School of Music, which he had cofounded with his brother Richard and others.

Despite these efforts, and more, Steve declined steadily. I began to end the treatments. My energy, however boundless, was no match for his disease. Even considering my willingness to exhaust my Gymboree bounty, my ability to help was fast approaching its outer limits. I was despondent and afraid. Roger, gently, told me he saw this as progress, because I was feeling the truth and making changes that fit the reality of my life circumstances. I was not so sure about that, but I understood.

My progress sometimes found legs when I was able to distract myself with how well YogaStudio was doing, a veritable silver lining. Nancy Evans operated like a consummate pro throughout my personal turbulence. We met for lunch a couple of times a week and I saw her in class. I stopped teaching during this time— too much to shoulder. Roger helped me see how I was living life on life's terms with maturity and purpose. He told me I was serving as a role model for my girls. I was not really thinking in those terms, but his acknowledgment and affirmations soothed my jagged nerves.

Roger helped me recognize how much affirming feedback could enhance relationships. Such experiences are a kind of alchemical reaction, as our brain releases serotonin when someone we love or respect affirms and acknowledges us with their graceful words. Of course, you don't need scientific data to know this for yourself. I tried to apply the same with Steve. I spoke to him several times a day about the sweetness I saw in him, naming specifics, and mirroring with words the range of positive feelings I experienced when with him. He beamed, his face lit up, and the temperature in the room would rise. Therein lay the potency of affirming love.

In the early days, Steve got lots of visits from his big circle of friends and family. For months I often came home to a house overflowing with people, filling the night with a party atmosphere. Amid the roar of blending margaritas, cranked music, and bellowed laughter and banter, I forgot that handsome Steve was no longer holding court with those gathered around him, as he had in times gone by. I wanted him to do it again, so I pretended he was. I, one of his daughters, or a caregiver would help him to bed while the cleanup proceeded with the same festive mood. In this way, I managed to keep myself from seeing too much of what I couldn't bear to see.

Then the visits waned. Dinner guests and drop-bys reduced to a trickle. The supportive community understandably returned their attention to their own lives, and I was compelled to face life with grim realism. Steve's measured speech was now more like that of a painfully reticent teen—one-word answers, shoulder shrugs, eyebrow raises, that sort of thing. He concealed the effort, but I knew that finding and expressing words made for a spirit-depleting struggle; stringing them together to make meaningful sentences was a relic of his past.

I had been well aware for months, maybe more than a year now, what others thought I "should" do. Steve did not fit easily into our active, sociable world. *Put him in a home.* That was standard operating procedure, was it not? Our nation tends to discard the diminished because they are weak, dependent, inconvenient. More than just averse, I was sickened by this idea. Having Steve's life in my hands, or at least so it seemed, was both daunting and focusing.

I consulted other spiritual leaders—Hindu teachers from my yogi world, rabbis from my Jewish background—and all the while Phillip Moffitt's words remained my guiding light. Nonetheless, I lacked any clear sense of what to do. Until I hired Rob to live with us in the separate outdoor guest suite, my home had been a revolving door of part-time care helpers. Even as wonderful Rob took on all daytime responsibilities, at night I transformed into a nurse, leaving me exhausted and depleted the next day. I wondered whether this pattern was sustainable.

I needed a break in the action. I devised a respite away, a trip with Steve to the Caribbean, a place for which I held a soft spot. I was reminded how in other countries, the marginalized are often a well-accepted part of family life, with everybody pitching in to make it work. Somehow I pictured an unassuming neighborhood on the blue Caribbean Sea, where I could care for Steve and get clear on next steps. This was a redux—with a twist—of my Cabin sabbatical after the Hasbro flip-flop.

I asked Rob if he wanted to join Steve and me for what I imagined would be a few months, most of which would not be a relaxing seashore holiday. Rob readily agreed. We shared a love of yoga and were becoming friends. Once abroad, Rob and I practiced yoga together on the condo deck. It strengthened our bond. We were a team of caretakers for Steve, as Steve required virtually constant supervision.

Steve was undemanding as he faded from us. He seemed more than content looking out at the aquamarine sea and the islands of Saba and St. Maarten in the distance while Rob and I spent a few hours in our yoga practice. Within a few days, we established a small community of friends on the remote Dieppe Bay, our home on the north end of St. Kitts. Most of the people we met there had never left the island. They fished for their food, harvested vegetables from their homegrown community garden near the sugarcane fields, and supplemented their meals by shinnying up coconut trees to grab the succulent fruits. They made money selling handmade crafts to the cruise ships that docked nearby a few days a week.

Dieppe Bay made for a grand adventure: we hosted a wedding for some local friends, dined with them every day, and became something of an extended family with their four children. I knew implicitly I could ask them for most anything. Basking in this Caribbean life, supported by Rob and our little community, I felt the looming ripeness of the time Phillip predicted would come. And it did. One morning as I sat on my yoga mat, I knew what I had to do, calling up words from a Mary Oliver poem, "The Journey": "One day you finally knew what you had to do . . . ."

I had to let go. I had to be more present for my daughters and other family members. I had to reinvest in the rest of my life. I told Rob the time had come to return to California and make arrangements to find a long-term care facility for Steve. I felt no equivocation. It had taken me more than a year to arrive here, and, as Phillip had predicted, I was good through and through, still unwaveringly committed to being Steve's steadfast champion all the way.

Once home, and after considerable research and numerous site visits, I found an assisted-living facility in San Francisco for Steve. I was confident this would the best place for him. It had excellent caretakers and a diverse community of residents whose circumstances precluded them, like Steve, from living on their own. Like Steve, many were relatively young, including his roommate, who was also in his mid-fifties.

A little space in my life opened. In May 2001, I was fortunate and honored to be present with my son-in-law, Shahir, when my daughter Cecily gave birth to my first grandchild, Ethan Blake. A month later, I placed Steve in the facility, which allowed me to travel comfortably to Santa Cruz and be with my grandson and my family. As Steve moved further away from me, I held new life in my arms. Beyond becoming "Noni," I began to spend more time helping to ensure Begin from Within stayed afloat. I returned my attention to YogaStudio. I became more social: went out to dinner, saw movies, attended concerts with friends, all of it.

Yet, lying on my bed at dusk one day, I struggled to turn a page in a novel I was reading. I was perplexed. I easily rationalized that dates with friends or family were acceptable reasons to be away from Steve at the care facility. But was staying at home to read a permissible excuse for my absence? Roger counseled that this "staying home" was the next and necessary step to reclaim my life and still know I was stalwart for Steve. We called it the "both/and." He suggested I make it a goal to stay home at least two nights a week and read a book, watch TV, or do whatever I chose. I accepted that placing Steve was not an end. Rather, it was just the next chapter of our life together. I had to find my way anew as both a business leader and a married woman living singly.

CHAPTER 19

∞∞∞∞∞∞∞∞∞∞∞∞∞∞∞∞∞∞∞∞∞∞∞∞

Listen In and Line Up

THEN CAME SEPTEMBER 11, 2001, and the world changed forever. As the shock lessened slightly, I sensed that greater access to yoga classes held strong value in bringing a semblance of peacefulness to the community in the wake of this horrific event. We reopened YogaStudio two days later on September 13. The tranquility inside our walls helped temper the prevailing sense of madness. The sanctuary of the yoga room, like the quiet place we seek inside ourselves, remained undisturbed by this horrific national tragedy. Students craved the calmness. Classes overflowed, and we had trouble making room for everyone. The overcapacity continued, then escalated. Most businesses understandably suffered in the aftermath of 9/11, but by the end of September,

YogaStudio had grown more than 20 percent. Like most, though, I still felt helpless, and I wanted to make some kind of lasting contribution. I decided I could help by opening a second studio to better serve the growing community of people turning to yoga during this difficult time, and at the same time I would be creating additional jobs. Expansion had never been my plan, but then 9/11 hadn't figured in anyone's plans. The new YogaStudio sister was larger and grander than the Mill Valley studio and located a few miles north in the town of Larkspur.

I entreated the spiritual leader Ram Dass, along with Phillip Moffitt, to give the invocation at our new location. Also a stroke survivor, Ram Dass had a connection to my husband Steve. Hundreds of yogis poured into the Larkspur studio. Some clustered on the couches and chairs, while most sat, yogi-style, on the available floor space in anticipation. We began with opening remarks, and the kinetic energy turned tranquil. Despite his stroke-induced difficulties, Ram Dass sat proudly upright in his wheelchair. Eventually, he signaled that he wished to speak. The studio lobby stilled to pin-drop silence, as he struggled to find words. Kind-hearted Phillip leaned down, put his arm around Ram Dass's shoulder, and they huddled. We witnessed these two masters interacting, moved by their compassion, presence, and love—three core yoga principles playing out in front of eager eyes. Phillip gestured to the group, which we understood meant that Ram Dass would do his best to be heard. If it were possible, the room grew quieter. Softly, just audibly, and ever so memorably, Ram Dass spoke: "This is a place to come cozy up to God."

There was a collective spontaneous chorus of soft gasping breaths. Spiritual or religious preferences aside, this reverent remark honored the purpose of all in attendance. In that moment, YogaStudio Larkspur officially opened.

I did not lose sight of the imprimatur of those two spiritual leaders, and how their presence would forever grace our foundation. Now, I had to focus my attention on the business to ground our good fortune. We kicked off with an extension of the charter membership program from the Mill Valley studio. Immediately, we had positive cash flow, as so many committed yogis elected for the monthly membership with our now en vogue auto deduct from their credit card.

In 2002, in another innovation, we combined a ground floor yoga studio location with a major retail presence in a trafficked shopping environment. Most yoga studios sit in offbeat (read, low rent) locations, with anything but mainstream friendly décor. We wanted our customers, and potential customers, to feel comfortable and welcomed in a grand lobby resembling an elegant hotel. The space allowed multiple purposes: relaxing, socializing, reading, waiting for class, enjoying tea, transacting business, and shopping. Some came just to shop. We joked that being in the calming space and sipping complimentary tea, while purchasing a lovely top, was as good as participating in a 90-minute yoga class. Well, not exactly.

We were on to something: put yoga where shoppers go and combine classes with a shopping experience in a calm, spacious waiting room. We made this happen in an environment where more than 50 students intermingled, patiently waiting for earlier classes to finish. The ambiance reflected our overall purpose, expressing calmness where chaos might otherwise prevail.

Word of mouth spread, and new students came without any advertising, as they had in the early days of Gymboree. A service business can mushroom when its high-touch quality really services. People felt both the benefits of the practice and the sense of inclusion and community, compelling their return, again and again, and propelling the business. Our overarching philosophy was that yoga held intrinsic value. That way we honored each student's desire for involvement. I was confident that the integrity of the practice was sufficient marketing. The impulse to come to class once or twice a week could morph naturally to four times weekly and often inspired an increase to six times a week. We did not want or generally have to push sales. Seeing the changes in your friend's temperament and body could be an enhancement to enroll, but sticking with yoga had to be experiential. Both were working.

We drew a variety of media coverage. In addition to yoga media outlets, which we had expected, we received the attention of print media ranging from design publications to business periodicals. Even "second act" stories appeared in the *Examiner*, *Chronicle*, and *Marin Independent Journal*, as well as nationally in *USA Today*. There was something appealing in the "Gymboree Lady's resurrection." People like to read about a rise from the ashes after a major crash and burn. These stories reassure us that tough times do not always end in final chapters featuring a fade into oblivion. I felt no hesitation about revealing the long haul I had experienced after leaving Gymboree, hitting the skids personally, and then climbing back to my second entrepreneurial opportunity with YogaStudio.

The media's attention continued. Comeback stories of women at midlife launching new careers or entrepreneurial ventures were hot. My story seemed fresh and had some complexity of flavor; again, unknowingly, I had arrived ahead of the curve.

It built from there. As the two studios began to show great promise, investors approached me. As opposed to the venture capitalists attracted to Gymboree, it was the yoga student community that wanted to put up their money. My idea was that the investors would make up a committed collective, each investing $100,000, for a total raise of between $750,000 and $1 million to fund the opening of a third studio. The longer-term vision was to raise more money after opening the third studio and create a Bay Area boutique group of as many as ten studios. While there were some firm commitments, this investment strategy had a ways to go before reaching critical mass. Old habits die hard; while I was cautious for obvious reasons owing to my history, the idea had me smitten.

Then, out of left field, a man named Richard Spencer, not a yogi himself, expressed interest in investing. There was, however, a hook. He wanted no other investors; he wanted the whole enchilada. While this hurled a monkey wrench into the current plan, I knew from experience that a solo investor could simplify things, and Richard assured me he would be hands-off.

As someone who knew bupkus about yoga, he got that I didn't want to be micromanaged.

I decided to move forward with Richard. When I told him I was ready to enter into an investment deal with him, however, he changed his tune. He no longer wanted to be all-in as an equity investor but wanted to hedge his $750,000 investment with conditions. Specifically, he wanted a deal structure that allowed him to exit the investment and get his money back according to an agreed formula if certain events occurred—essentially, what's called a "put option." As we negotiated, Richard wanted so many different events to trigger his right to exercise the "put" that I became frustrated. I realized he wanted too much of the cake to eat himself. He wanted virtually no risk and all upside. I told him, "How about you can get out of the equity investment for any reason whatsoever, on your whim, but only within three years of signing? That way, the put option has a three-year term, after which, if not earlier exercised, you can no longer exit the investment and must become a committed equity investor. I want to know I have a committed partner, not someone who can pull out at any point."

I was not crazy about the put option, even with the modification I proposed. I knew well from my Gymboree days that the motivations of investors and founders often diverge. But I had little choice at this point; he would likely walk if I didn't agree, and the other investment opportunities had not coalesced. We made the deal.

And so it went. Before long, we opened our third studio in San Francisco. By 2006, YogaStudio was a family of three upscale, spa-like yoga centers with a staff of 75 yoga teachers and 20 administrative personnel. Our locations were in highly populated locations and were beautiful—even winning a design award, shades of Gymboree's similar feat with its retail store award some 20 years prior! We expanded our yoga clothing boutiques, offered numerous international travel retreats, and created partnerships with spa and massage outlets. The bountiful amenities, including yoga gear, yoga-to-street wear, jewelry, books, and DVDs, rounded out the distinctive environment.

YogaStudio tapped into a unique community that ranged from dedicated and advanced yogis to novices of all types and ages. We spoke to all of them and blurred traditional submarket distinctions. We created a lifestyle brand through the development of a product line and a healthy way of life. We helped move yoga from fringe to mainstream in the Bay Area, a trend that Yoga Works in Los Angeles had also advanced. My aspiration was to shape a business that thrived on the foundations of yogic tradition, and, with honor and respect, bring that alive in a community-based commercial world. The *New York Times* best-selling author Laura Fraser did a feature story on me in the "Second Acts" column of the national women's magazine *More*. The article prompted *The Today Show* to call. Financial correspondent Anne Thompson, with camera crew shooting at each pit stop, visited our San Francisco studio, traveled to my Mill Valley home, and hiked with me through the woods, after which we met my daughters at the Pacific Ocean. The result: a six-minute piece about me, Gymboree, my bulimia and recovery, and the building of a community way of life through YogaStudios.

Richard loved the national media surge. He was convinced we had hit a tipping point. But as I had learned from the Gymboree experience, media adulation did not necessarily equate to financial success, especially as defined by investors. Our P&L was not as rosy as the media glorification would have suggested. Richard was disappointed that the media attention did not translate to the bottom line. We were in the middle of the third year of his investment.

Richard invited me to what I thought would just be one of our semi-regular lunch/update sessions. Without much ado, he matter-of-factly exercised the put, as was his prerogative. I was crushed. I had to capitulate, even though the business had enormously happy customers (yet again, just like Gymboree) and held much promise. In those respects, we seemed to be flourishing. But our inconsistent profits meant I would soon need funds to keep us afloat. And, on top of it all, I now had to scramble to find a way to buy Richard out.

What had I gotten myself into? What had happened to my idea for a simple, individual studio resembling a modest Gymboree franchise? After some more self-flagellation, I moved into action. I sourced the funds by refinancing my home and bought Richard out pronto. Next, I cut expenses while I figured out a longer-term strategy. How much more Gymboree flashback could I manage?

Allison Berardi, our general manager, and Michelle Fliegauf, who handled our workshops and retreats, were also investors and remained committed during these hard times. They were exemplary employees who believed we could turn YogaStudio around. But I was finding it intolerable to watch my savings depleted to meet monthly payroll, worried that I had just enough to Band-Aid the bleeding that portended hemorrhage.

I was at a major business crossroads. Should I stay in the game or sell YogaStudio? Potential new investors wanted me to remain so they could possibly fund the original idea to develop a San Francisco Bay chain. And there was a prospective suitor in Yoga Works, the only national yoga chain that (in my opinion) had both an impressive CEO, Phil Swain, and a reputation for being well respected in the yoga community. Phil was brilliant, super likable, a true leader, and as skillful and natural a communicator as I had ever come across. The possibility of an association with Phil was appealing. I also had to consider the interests of the other investors beyond Allison and Michelle. I spoke to other potential buyers, including some I met through business brokers, and to my brother, Michael Greengard, himself a national business broker. Mike had been the first board member at YogaStudio and was my trusted ally. He knew the business inside and out, and his counsel was informed by his pedigreed Ivy League education and MBA. More, as an entrepreneur himself with the experience of countless mergers and acquisitions under his belt, he knew well the pitfalls on the road to the sale of a business. He helped me weigh the various options and stay focused on a timely and well-considered decision. I was all too familiar with how things can go sideways en route to a final deal, and his sage advice was invaluable.

From a different perspective, I was in the middle of rebuilding my life with and without Steve. Cecily was expecting another child. Meegan was back from New York and living in San Francisco. Spending time with my family was a priority. I was also involved in a new romantic relationship that had started a year after I placed Steve in the care facility (and lasted more than two years). It worked for me in a way that did not impinge on my loyalty to Steve, despite the stark reality that my love for Steve would forever more be unrequited. I remained committed to being Steve's sustaining steward. I also faced having to move Steve again, as his steady decline made it impossible for him to stay at his current care facility in San Francisco. He now needed a full-on nursing home. Steve's brother Richard found a wonderful place for him in LA, where Richard and the other Strauss family members lived, and I agreed. I continued to fund his care, with generous assistance from his mother, and on some level I was relieved that after nearly a decade, the daily care focus would shift to Richard.

Meanwhile I had much to consider about YogaStudio, especially as the cash kept pouring out of my personal accounts. By this time, in 2008, I had spent more than eleven years building up this vibrant yoga community and was by far the major financial player. We had expensive long-term leases in my name. This was complicated. Did I have it in me to figure it out, assuming a solution could be found? The economy had taken a downward turn, although none of us knew how serious it would become. I focused on some available short-term solutions, but all involved major salary cuts and a complete restructuring of teacher compensation; I was not prepared for a staff walkout. Could I even find a reasonable buyer? Would a sell decision mean "success," and, if so, what kind? How would it affect the others—investors, staff, students? Could I sell and still retain the respect of the flourishing yoga community?

This time, unlike the period that led to my Gymboree departure, I had good access to myself and what mattered to me. I took a deep breath—many deep breaths—and drew heavily from the unforgettable lessons of the Gymboree days. Eventually, the same powerful words of Phillip Moffitt worked for me in this situation. I lined up to knowing myself and declined to expand the business any further. Most of the potential buyers fell by the wayside or proved untimely, and I thrust my energy into forging a deal with Yoga Works. As we approached 2009, with the world economy in a major slide, Yoga Works acquired my three YogaStudio locations and I largely cashed out, retaining a modest stock position in Yoga Works and agreeing to a yearlong consulting agreement.

The core truth was that I had come to know when the jig was up—for me. I had learned to "listen in" and have the courage to act accordingly. I knew that my true preference was to focus *on* my yogi life, not being *in* the yoga business. The stresses, even the highs, I realized, came under the umbrella of adrenaline rush, and I had lost the taste for that. My nervous system had been honed by my years of yoga practice to thrive in the more temperate climates of ease and serenity. I saw myself as someone who, on her good days, managed to live in moderation.

CHAPTER 20

⌐◇◇◇◇◇◇◇◇◇◇◇◇◇◇◇◇◇◇◇◇◇◇◇◇◇⌐

Build Your Own Table

"SO, HOW ARE YOU FEELING ABOUT ALL THIS? This is a pretty big deal, isn't it, selling your business to Yoga Works?"

These questions came from a fellow yogi who had joined with other yogis and friends at my home to celebrate the Yoga-Studio sale. I wasn't sure I was up for a personal debriefing on the range of my feelings right at that moment.

"Thanks for asking. I feel pretty good, although I am still taking it all in."

"What's next for you?"

"Ha. Good question. Right now, I think I will kick back and see what the settling dust brings. I'll watch my thoughts—you know, real yogi-style." This managed to deflect further questions, and as the exchange ended the celebration rose up around us.

The next morning predictably found me indulging my usual urge to restore my home to its pre-party state, all serving platters properly placed in their cupboard dwellings, glassware hand dried, and recycling out at the curb. After order was restored, the house went quiet, and I was left alone with my thoughts. I grabbed a sweatshirt to protect against the morning chill and moved with soft steps to the courtyard outside to sit. As I reminisced in silence, I returned to the two provocative questions put to me at the party.

How was I feeling about the sale of the business? In truth, I had much pride and no regrets. I was proud of our business innovations and of how we had contributed to the local employment market, especially for women. I was proud of the vibrant way the business had connected to the larger community and proud of how it had sprouted its own community subculture. Foremost, I was proud I had built a business that lined up with who I had become. And I was equally satisfied that when the business put my internal balance at risk, I had been able to let it go.

I had embraced, embodied, and chosen to live by the yoga philosophy that our wisest teacher is found inside each of us. This freed me to prioritize my personal life over my business. It did not mean I was without a sensation of bittersweetness about the colleagues and other people I had left behind, or had no attachments to my former life, or had no fears about my future. I had those feelings. My main focus was being at peace with myself, secure in the knowledge that I had made the right decision for me, despite a less than desirable financial outcome. I needed to play it forward, and I did—a momentous decision I could not have made in my Gymboree days.The community-minded yoga business would continue to live on in me whether or not I was at the helm. I likened it to those great loves in our lives that never die because they become part of us. As I contemplated the wonderful run I'd had with YogaStudio—the student community, the staff, the yoga, the union of all of it—I felt increasingly grateful.

So, then, what was next? The immediate next stage was far from retirement. Call it a respite, a period in which new directions would take time to appear in ways that felt right for me. Stated more aptly in the currency of the day, it would be a "re-invention transition." With a welcome-wagon attitude, I hoped to beckon, and reckon with, my entreprencurial muse.

As I bided my time, 2010 marked the endpoint of an agreement I had made with my therapist Roger: to stay in my Mill Valley house for ten years after placing Steve in his first care facility upon our return from the Caribbean. In the fifteen years since my relocation back to Mill Valley, I had done the following: built a nonprofit in Begin from Within; made a second entrepreneurial run with YogaStudio, followed by a sale of that business; embarked on a second marriage that had made a sharp, tragic turn; rebuilt relations with my daughters; seen the birth of three grandchildren; and maintained a durable recovery from my addictions.

Now, I decided to sell my Mill Valley house, and I moved to a tiny condo in San Francisco. I felt tinges of apprehension like a coed off to a huge college campus, excited to find my way. It was the first time I had ventured out armed with a well-grounded sense of me. That move was my move, and it excited me.

In an irony not lost on me, I chose to live a few blocks from the assisted-living facility in the Hayes Valley neighborhood of San Francisco where Steve had spent almost a decade. I felt comfortable there, and maybe there was some unconscious closeness and healing I needed from the proximity. While Steve lived in a nursing home in LA now, I often felt him there. I had vivid memories of our frequent wheelchair strolls in Hayes Valley, as we watched its gentrification unfold. While I was into my new day-to-day life, Steve was omnipresent, living quietly inside me.

The diagnosis doctors had given Steve twelve years ago came true. By 2010, he was immobile, spoke infrequently, and what he knew or did not know was anyone's guess. My visits had decreased from daily, at first, to every six months during the previous year or two. Visits began to follow a pattern. As I entered his room and saw him, I would smile broadly and say, "Hello, good looking. How're you doing today?"

I would search for movement in his eyes, some sign that my words reached a part of him. He saw someone, but it was not clear he recognized me or comprehended my words.

I would approach him, place my hands on each of his shoulders, squeeze softly, and kiss him on the forehead, whispering, "Good morning."

I would step back to scan his face for any sign of response or recognition. There would not be much, if any. Gone were the days when he would summon the strength and clarity of mind to say, "Hey Red," his nickname for me.

I would grab a chair and rearrange it so I could sit across from him, never losing eye contact, and share an important current story, as Steve was a news junkie. He would move slightly in his hospital bed, tilted upright so I could see his eyes, yet not so erect he risked tipping over. He lacked the ability to hold himself up without support. I interpreted any upward gesture in his eyes as a request to come closer. I would lean in, hear his breath, feel his mass. As my body would approach his, I would see his face soften a little, I think. I sensed (or imagined) he was trying to identify me by smell.

People would ask me, "Does he know you?" This question always seemed to me like a way to get a bead on his level of decline. For their part, doctors could only surmise and speculate. Most professionals believed that his cognitive function was exceedingly minimal, but those opinions were inherently imprecise. His best friend since college, Robbie Long, interacted with him, or so it seemed, in ways that belied professional belief. Who knew, really? I hoped he felt my presence in some warm way that brightened his day, even for a moment or two.

Steve held a kind of dignity about his world, reduced to his bed, chair, and the bulletin board full of photos I assembled for him. On a small shelf sat some of his favorite books, which he could not hold, let alone read, and photos of the musicians he admired. These comrades seemed to comfort him. We who loved him continued to tell his story.

I would read him excerpts from his books, including some Ginsberg poetry, and show him beloved photos of his days as an active student participant in the free-speech movement at UC Berkeley during the 1960s. When I showed him the pictures, his eyes barely scanned.

Part of the time, we would just hang out, he in a world I couldn't enter or know and me reading or watching him. It was a different kind of coexistence. After a while, I would play some of his favorite music. One time, during a Muddy Waters riff, he puckered his lips as if to kiss. Could it be? Who cared—I went for it. I stood up, put my arms securely around him, and kissed him. When I sat down, I felt tears dripping down my cheeks. He was unaffected on the surface.

As odd as it sounds, he seemed content. Was that because I was there, or was it his new natural state, like a Buddha, centered and clear, without fret or worry? While feeling helpless would seem natural, I felt differently. I knew there was little I could do, which framed my expectations. I did what felt right, knowing that whatever light I cast became our shared gift and the appropriate measure of what I could do. This understanding comforted me.

Steve's life ended peacefully at the age of 66. I scattered some of his ashes in the Pacific Ocean at Stinson Beach in Marin County, where he and I had spent many Saturdays tossing a tennis ball in a lame attempt at keep-away from his dog Milo. As I walked off the beach after the ash-spreading ceremony, astonishingly, I ran into Philip Moffitt—yes, the same Phillip Moffitt whose sage advice had sustained me and who I had not seen for years. Phillip was coming onto the beach right as I was coming off. I told him what I had just done a moment ago. He smiled, and kept nodding while speaking a few kind words. He needed no reminder of his prescient counsel of more than a decade before.

As I regrouped, I took on meaningful volunteer work. I taught weekly yoga classes to incarcerated women in the San Francisco women's jail. We became a little sangha (community) where yoga practice helped soften the corrosiveness of distrust. Their work ethic, desire to grow, and spirit brightened my world. I decided to do some more direct service work and became a spiritual care partner (a cousin of hospice care), at the Jewish Home of San Francisco. My work 20 years before with the Home's Alzheimer's day care center in Miami, as I transitioned from the Pathways treatment center, felt unfinished. While Steve had gone through similar stages as some Alzheimer's patients, I wanted to better understand humanity during this period of life, and have a better sense of my own humility. I felt a sense of completion. The service work was a counterpoint to the building stages I'd gone through in my life.

In 2012, after less than two years in my city dwelling, I felt the call to return to Mill Valley. I missed living at the base of Mt. Tamalpais, where I could easily do my daily hikes on her myriad trails. While grateful for the adventure of my city time, I sold my condo and purchased a place back in my adopted hometown. I was jazzed to take up a regular routine, especially one that included "adventure days with Noni" with each of my three grandchildren. These were precious times.

As I settled in, modest next-act trial runs trickled to my doorstep. I was asked to speak at various conferences across the nation, including as a keynote speaker at several women's conferences and entrepreneurial events. This was uplifting work, as I experienced heartfelt reactions to my story. It was also too draining and isolating to consider doing this any more than several times a year. I was not attracted to a life of speaking many times a month, traveling to cities far and wide, despite flattering invitations and encouragement. And so I waited for something to grab me as passionately as Gymboree and YogaStudio had ensnared me. I knew well the difference between something I enjoyed and something that "had" me.

I joined a panel of a national angel investor network that reviewed funding requests for cutting-edge businesses at the seed (incubation) stage, kind of like a pre-*Shark Tank* investment candidate review. As panelists, we studied PowerPoint presentations, prepared for in-person recaps, and, after in-person presentations, asked what I hoped were insightful questions. The panel Q&A occurred in San Francisco in front of avid live audiences numbering several hundred, and included potential investors, curious entrepreneurs, and other professionals working in related industries. I met many starry-eyed, capable young entrepreneurs, which generated invitations for additional keynote speaking engagements and potential consulting gigs.

I began to focus on mentoring and advising female entrepreneurs. This seemed like a sweet spot for me: working with young women to help give life and focus to their visions. Budding entrepreneurs habitually seek out regular advisers, mentors, coaches, and senior guides to assist in securing seed money or additional investment capital raises, a resource not available to me when I started Gymboree and YogaStudio. These young women—bright, focused, passionate, and dogged—inspired me with a thrilling sense of what could be. I fit their bill for a welcome cheerleader and coach.

Their youthful fervor fascinated me, and I saw my younger self in them. There was something beautiful in our multigenerational connection, much as there had been at YogaStudio with Allison and Michelle and (the older) me, and at Gymboree with Bud Jacob and (the younger) me. Businesses have so much to gain from intergenerational insights, and they can suffer when leaders hire staff who are carbon copies of one another.

Then the Nasdaq Entrepreneurial Center opened in San Francisco across the street from Gymboree corporate headquarters. As a prelaunch, Nasdaq initiated a program for casting-call applicants for season 7 of *Shark Tank*, a favorite show of mine, and I was invited to join the elite "Prep Panel" to assist in the selection process. I could not have been more thrilled. Our job was to critique dry-run pitches and provide feedback, tips, and guidance in anticipation of their actual money pitch later in the day. The give-and-take dynamics were exhilarating and inspiring. This harked back to another Stuart Moldaw legacy: when your bus comes by, jump on it, for opportunity may be on the route.

In September 2015, the Nasdaq Entrepreneurial Center held an official opening, which included current CEOs of NASDAQ companies. The turnout was impressive, a veritable who's who of Bay Area business leadership. To my surprise, for the opening, the Center invited me to represent Gymboree, a proud NASDAQ member for seventeen years, even though the company is now private, and I had never been CEO when it was public. I accepted with humility and appreciation of the significant honor to be recognized by NASDAQ as Gymboree's delegate. The mission of the Center is to support the entrepreneur at every stage of the journey: conception, launch, fund-raising, setbacks, repositioning, exiting, reinvention, and so on.

I am now part of a select group of thought leaders at the Nasdaq Entrepreneurial Center, where I will create, curate, and lead events and panels with the assistance of their programming team to advance its mission. I am stoked to see where this can go as a potential next act in the entrepreneurial ride.

I embrace life as it is and as it comes. For now, I'm comfortable with mentoring and advising, select speaking engagements, yoga, hikes, matriarch responsibilities, meaningful friendships, and family relationships. In them, I have balance, contentment, and a sense of purpose that lines up well with who I am. My internal voices, while not always in equipoise, now operate respectfully together. They team up with my enhanced patience and moderation, and reduced impulsiveness, to make time my friend and to size up any potential paths to play it forward. I hope you do, too.

EPILOGUE

Completing the Circle

AFTER GYMBOREE FLOURISHED as a public company for seventeen years, in 2010, Bain Capital took the company I started with $3,000 in seed money private for $1.8 billion. Based in San Francisco, Gymboree now operates more than 1,200 specialty retail stores of children's apparel in the United States, Puerto Rico, and Canada, and it has nearly 650 franchised play-and-music centers worldwide.

The acquisition of YogaStudio gave Yoga Works a foothold in Northern California, with 21 yoga studios and plans for more growth on the drawing board. After adding several studios in the ensuing years, in June 2015, Yoga Works acquired San Francisco–based Yoga Tree and its eight yoga studios. The acquisition and

recent expansion increased its presence to more than 50 locations across Northern California, Southern California, New York,
Boston, Baltimore, and Washington, D.C. Yoga Works plans to
continue its expansion.

I would not turn back the clock for any increment of time.
While both companies are, by any measure, financial success stories, the experiences I had with them hold primary value for me
in the unforgettable and lasting lessons, challenges, and opportunities that defined and refined me. Today, I enjoy with fondness and contentment the paths both businesses traveled and
where they wound up, much in the way parents revel in the even-
tual adulthood of their children. For my part, what I endured in
creating and leading these wonderful businesses, the lucky and
unlucky, tough and easy, up and down, silly and sad, and joy and
consternation, was all exquisite work. They gave me a robust gift.

ACKNOWLEDGMENTS

WE WERE GRACED to have access to an ensemble of inestimable professionals who early on taught us the ropes of the publishing world, including Megan Casey, Peggy Northrop, Laura Fraser, Adrian Zackheim, Susan Moldaw, Maria Gagliano, Elizabeth Kaplan, Amy Rennert, Liza Dawson, Toni Sciarra Poynter, and Bonnie Solow.

We extend special thanks to our steadfast and wise champion Robert Stricker.

We praise our loyal and ever-believing agents at Trident Media Group, Melissa Flashman and Ellen Levine, and their able colleagues, Sara Pearl, Allisyn Shindle, Alyssa Cami, Alexa Stark, and Sarah Bush.

We tip our hats to our wonderfully talented developmental editor, Stuart Horwitz.

We bow to our extraordinary book editor, Doug Seibold at Agate Publishing, who wowed us with his uncommon sensibility and craftsmanship, and his talented and tireless team of Zach Rudin, Eileen Johnson, Jacqueline Jarik, and Morgan Krehbiel.

We cannot thank enough our dear friends Bonnie Dahan and Stephen Yafa, for their unwavering wisdom, advice, and compassion as we navigated this process.

Michael thanks his sons, Torin and Aidan Coffino, and his siblings, Dianne Coffino, Theresa Coffino, Joanie Marrazzo, and John Coffino, for staying on him forever to launch a writing career, and his lifelong Bronx buddies Donald Kuhnert, Tommy O'Leary, Joe Lynch, Jack Fitzgerald, and Bob Rice for personifying loyal friendship.

Joan keeps a special place in her heart for her sisterhood of girlfriends, including Julie Allison, Michelle Esrick, Denise Kaufman, Margaret O'Leary, Max Lampert, Andrea Blum, Sue Siegel, and Lori B, beaming stars who brightened her life each day of the book journey.

Joan thanks Lisa Shanower, Charity Tooze, Julie Gordon White, Stephanie Shaterian, and Maureen Birdsall for their appreciable professional contributions.

We acknowledge the countless Gymboree families, franchisees, board members, staff, yogis, and colleagues who embody the soul and spirit of this book. There are too many to mention and so we honor them all through these distinguished delegates:

Nancy Bott, Linda Rasmussen, Karen Anderson, Julie Arvan, Bud Jacob, Bob Campbell, Linda Brownstein, the late Stuart Moldaw and George Gaber, Carolyn André, Donny and Adrian Becker, Coni Goudie, Debbie Whitefield, Jackie Dyer, Nancy Evans, Rob Horsley, Michael Greengard, Allison Berardi, Michelle Fliegauf, Phillip Moffitt, Ram Dass, and Phil Swain.

With respect and gratitude, we acknowledge the creative Gymboree team that worked closely with us on this project— Mark Breitbard, Jill Johnson, Gena Segno, Dawn Sagorski, Alison McGlone, Parnell Eagle—as well as the Nasdaq Entrepreneurial Center, and the brilliant Elana Rosen Yonah and Celena Aponte, for hosting us as authors-in-residence and staging a special book launch event.

Special thanks to Jessica Palopoli for her exquisite cover photography.

We again thank those who blessed us with testimonials: Peggy Northrop, Rachel Pally, Elana Yonah Rosen, Phil Swain, Patricia Ziegler, Susan Griffin-Black, Karen Behnke, Stephanie Brenner Kirksey, Chip Conley, Phillip Moffitt, Yvonne Hao, and Rieva Lesonsky.

And last, but not least, we thank each other for the love, resilience, hard work, patience, compassion, endurance, belief, and understanding that produced a remarkably (well, relatively) smooth ride getting this book done.

ABOUT THE AUTHORS

JOAN BARNES founded and served as CEO of Gymboree, an international network of franchised play programs and company-owned retail stores. For more than a decade, Barnes was the principal owner of San Francisco–based YogaStudio, which helped to mainstream the "yoga lifestyle." She also founded Begin from Within through the Jewish Family and Children's Services of San Francisco, which features programs dedicated to people with food, weight, and body-image issues.

MICHAEL COFFINO spent 36 years as a successful business litigator, trial attorney, writing coach, and mentor to young attorneys. During his legal career, he was a trusted adviser to CEOs, boards of directors, and general counsels of public companies. Born in the Bronx, Coffino graduated from the City University of New York with a BS in education and went on to earn his JD from the University of California, Berkeley, School of Law.